The Supreme Celebration & Bylove of Word

The Supreme Celebration & Bylove of Word

KING SOLOMON SPIRITUAL LIBRARY
THE GOD ENCYCLOPAEDIA WORD OF INFINITY

BY
THE SPIRIT OF THE FATHER GOD
THROUGH HIS SERVANT
HRM KING SOLOMON DAVID JESSE ETE
(King Solomon Spiritual Library)
Eteroyal Universal Family - BCS

All rights reserved
Copyright © Solomon ETE, 2008
Solomon ETE is hereby identified as author of this work in accordance with Section 77 of the Copyright, Designs and Patents Act 1988

The book cover picture is copyright to Solomon ETE

This book is published by
King Solomon Spiritual Library
P O BOX 27394
London E12 6WW UK
www.ksslibrary.com
www.kingsolomonspirituallibrary.com

This book is sold subject to the conditions that it shall not, by way of trade or otherwise, be lent, resold, hired out or otherwise circulated without the author's or publisher's prior consent in any form of binding or cover other than that in which it is published and without a similar condition including this condition being imposed on the subsequent purchaser.

A CIP record for this book is available from the British Library
ISBN 978-0-9559801-1-4

THE UNIVERSAL INVITATION

= = = =

You Are Invited To Join Me In THE UNIVERSAL SUPREME WORD SEASON CELEBRATION And Celebrate; Acknowledge, Appreciate and give full RECOGNITION to
THE UNIVERSAL SUPREME WORD,
YOUR LIFE, THE FORCE OF ALLTHINGS, THE TOTALITY OF ALL TOTALITIES YOUR CREATOR,
THE SUPREME FATHER GOD ALMIGHTY,
THE CREATOR OF THE UNIVERSE Wherever You Be.

The Supreme Celebration & Bylove of Word

EVERY 1ST OCTOBER TO 10TH OCTOBER YEARLY

===

Published by:
KING SOLOMON SPIRITUAL LIBRARY
ETEROYAL UNIVERSAL FAMILY
IKOT OKWO, ETE COMMUNITY
IKOT ABASI L.G.A
AKWA IBOM STATE OF NIGERIA
WEST AFRICA

WWW.KSSLIBRARY.COM
WWW.COME4WORD.COM
WWW.THEWORDCITY.COM
WWW.KINGSOLOMONSPIRITUALLIBRARY.COM

Contact EMAIL:
hrmkingsolomon@eteroyalmail.com

THANK YOU FATHER

Preface of THE FATHER'S TALK (GOD PRESENT)

In the name of Our Lord Jesus Christ
In the blood of Our Lord Jesus Christ
Now and forever more, Amen

As **I** always say, let every human heart be clean and clear and be with humility and understanding with LOVE to hear from **THE FATHER GOD** once again. If you have this faith and that belief then, the communication between you and **I** will flow very well. However, if you withhold your heart from **ME THE FATHER GOD** by hiding yourself and having a double mind due to doubts and not believing in **ME**, then the communication of understanding will be influenced by your thoughts as you do not believe **THE FATHER GOD**. That is the reason **I** bring all manners of information and explanations about **THE FATHER'S TALK (GOD PRESENT)**.

I want you to believe that **THE FATHER'S TALK (GOD PRESENT)** information is NOT motivated by cunning or by the human mind. It is NOT the WORD from a studio of carnality. It is NOT a broadcast by evil or by the second thought of a human being. **THE FATHER'S TALK (GOD PRESENT)** information is a direct broadcast, straight from **THE FATHER GOD**. They are broadcasted directly from the studio of **THE FATHER GOD ALMIGHTY THE SUPREME WORD OF THE UNIVERSE.**

All **THE FATHER'S TALK (GOD PRESENT)** Lecture Revelations are direct from **THE FATHER GOD ALMIGHTY THE CREATOR OF THE UNIVERSE,** why **THE FATHER'S TALK (GOD PRESENT)** always mention as Lecture Revelation is because you do not need anyone to interpret any **WORD** of **THE FATHER'S TALK (GOD PRESENT)** to you. That is why **I** call this WISDOM, '**BEYOND THE HUMAN KNOW**'.

When **I EXIST, I WAS, WAS, WAS**, this information was in existence with **ME** and that means that indirectly, **I THE FATHER GOD ALMIGHTY THE SUPREME WORD OF THE UNIVERSE, AM** revealing **MYSELF** to humankind once again. **I** do this so that you would not continue to think that **I THE FATHER GOD** does not speak directly with human beings anymore. And most importantly, this **FATHER'S TALK (GOD PRESENT)** Lecture Revelations are NOT via any angel. They are not inspirational outcomes from one possessed by an angel or a ghost. They are directly from *"**THE SUPREME SILENT THOUGHT OF CREATION**"*, **THE FATHER GOD'S** 'POSSESSING HEART' **THE UNIVERSAL SUPREME WORD. I**

TAKE OVER THE BODY, THE SOUL AND SPIRIT OF His Royal Majesty KING SOLOMON DAVID JESSE **ETE** the incarnated King Solomon David of Israel who was also incarnate ABEL the second positive son of Adam THAT **I** NOW TALK THROUGH.

This particular Lecture Revelation that points out that this is **Beyond What Human Know** serves as a preface to all **THE FATHER'S TALK** (**GOD PRESENT**) Lecture Revelations. This information should come before the main Lecture Revelation. You know that you are not reading the words of the chairman of your local council or the words of the leader of your church or the words of a president or a prime minister or the words of any human being. This information is called **THE FATHER'S TALK** (**GOD PRESENT**) because it comes directly from **ME THE FATHER GOD THE CREATOR OF THE UNIVERSE**.

THE FATHER GOD ALMIGHTY is the **SPIRIT** that motivated **THE WORD**, that created **THE WORD** and made **THE WORD** come to be in existence and this is the **SPIRIT** that is talking now as **THE FATHER'S TALK (GOD PRESENT)**.

The reason **I AM** bringing this particular short **FATHER'S TALK (GOD PRESENT)** Lecture Revelation, is so that when you read, **THE FATHER'S TALK (GOD PRESENT)** Lecture Revelations or listen to any of them by accessing them in anyway, do not attribute them to ordinary vision or prophesy. This is not a discussion but a Revelation Information from the **Archive Record**, THE KING SOLOMON SPIRITUAL LIBRARY- **The Boom Heart of THE FATHER GOD** where all the information is kept. It is only when and how **I** want the information to come that the information will come.

It is not a case of starting to think about what to say and what to write or doing a research. Therefore, when you read or listen to any of **THE FATHER'S TALK (GOD PRESENT)** Lecture Revelations and you don't believe, then at the end of the day, you have yourself to blame.

WHAT IS THIS AGAIN

When **I** searched in the Spiritual Supreme Memory of **MYSELF**, which is where all hearts of human beings came from by creation, the percentage of seventy-five percent ask this question in spirit: **What Is This Again**? In other words they are asking where the information came from. Who brings them out? That is why **I AM** bringing out this particular information to answer the question. It means that most of all hearts that is, seventy-five percent of all the hearts are asking **THE FATHER GOD**, **What Is This Again**.

This **FATHER'S TALK (GOD PRESENT)** Lecture Revelation title is ***AFTER THOSE DAYS SAYS THE***

LORD MOST HIGH prophesied by Isaiah.

AFTER THOSE DAYS SAYS THE LORD MOST HIGH is THE TESTIMONY OF EVERLASTING **WORD, EVERLASTING SUPREME WORD OF THE FATHER GOD**, AND THE TESTIMONY OF **THE HOLY SPIRIT OF TRUTH** PERSONIFIED ON EARTH.

When **I** attended to this job physically and finished it, **I** had to keep the record of **MY** WORK and the record could not come direct from **MY** human person personified. It had to come from The **Servant** as the **Witness**. And that Servant and the Witness must be motivated and interacted together with **ME** so that whatever He would say will not come from the human mind but will come from the heart of **THE FATHER GOD**. This **Servant** and **Witness** is His Royal Majesty (HRM) King Solomon David Jesse **ETE**. He is **MY Servant** and **Witness** that **I AM** directly involved with from the time of The

Beginning when **I LIVED BEYOND THE HUMAN KNOW**.

BEYOND THE HUMAN KNOW is before creations.

BEYOND THE HUMAN KNOW is before even the SOUND that manifested THE SPOKEN WORD, a formulation by **ME THE FATHER GOD** in the '*hidinan'* – the centre where the sound formed '**GEN**' OF LIFE in the middle of the A*kwavor.*

Akwavor is where **I** generated **MYSELF** on top of the water. You will see most of this information in other **FATHER'S TALK (GOD PRESENT)** Lecture Revelation.

Where **I** generated **MYSELF** and formed the steam of **MY** energy on top of the water is called *akwavor.* And **MY** energy brought out the sound and then the water from the steam rushed back to the **deep** called *Odu Idem Abasi*. When the water was rushing back to *Odu Idem Abasi,* the rushing force generated the sound and the energy of the sound produced the **Gen** of **THE SPOKEN WORD "THE CREATOR"**. And this place called ***Odu Idem Abasi*** (THE HARDWARE OF THE SPIRIT) is where the rushing force of energy of creation comes from and goes back before the sun breaks out the following day. That is why **I AM** telling you that this information titled **BEYOND THE HUMAN KNOW** therefore **THE FATHER'S TALK (GOD PRESENT)** information is beyond the sphere of human beings. That is, the information that existed before the existence of creation.

There was nothing like human beings and there was nothing like souls. But there was something as something called **SOMETHING, THE SUPREME THOUGHT (THE DIVINE LOVE THE UNIVERSAL SUPREME WORD)** that eventually came to be born as Our Lord Jesus Christ. That is the potency **I** used to create Adam and lived in Adam, as **I THE FATHER'S TALK (GOD PRESENT)**. When **I** say **THE FATHER'S TALK**

(**GOD PRESENT**), I mean I, -**THIS SUPREME WORD**. So, that is the answer to the question that seventy-five percent of the human souls ask as '**What Is This Again?**'

    This is EVERLASTING TESTIMONY ABOUT THE **SUPREME WORD OF THE UNIVERSE, THE PERSONIFIED HOLY SPIRIT OF TRUTH**. This is the last information that humankind will live with by from **THE FATHER GOD AND IS LIVED BY THE FATHER GOD**. From **THE FATHER GOD** live by **THE FATHER GOD** and with **THE FATHER GOD ALMIGHTY**. Then everything will be **THE FATHER GOD! THE FATHER GOD! THE FATHER GOD! FATHER! FATHER! FATHER GOD ALMIGHTY**! Call no one FATHER except **THE SUPREME FATHER**. Of all the human beings on earth, it is one person that is **THE FATHER**. Also of the humans on earth it is only one person that is **the Servant**. These are the representative of the **THOUGHT** and the **WORD**. The body where those two things live called Adam is **THE KING OF KINGS AND THE LORD OF LORDS**. So, you have one **FATHER** and one **LORD** and that is **THE KING OF KINGS** and **THE LORD OF LORDS**. Every other person is a servant of **THE FATHER GOD** that is, sons and daughters of **THE FATHER GOD**. Therefore, with this Revelation you don't need to ask, **'What Is This Again'**.

You know, yesterday, today and tomorrow **I AM** the same and because of that, you will NEVER know the way of **THE FATHER GOD** because the more you look the less you see.

THIS IS INFORMATION OF THE FATHER GOD ALMIGHTY

This is not information of your father, your brother, your sister, your mother, your husband, your wife, your president, your King, your Queen or yourself. It is not! **THIS IS INFORMATION FROM THE FATHER GOD ALMIGHTY, THE CREATOR OF**

THE UNIVERSE. It is NOT from angel. So, when you are reading or listening to the information clarify your heart.

In fact, **I** have said this time without number that the number of people and the human beings that will show respect whenever they come across **THE FATHER'S TALK** (**GOD PRESENT**) Lecture Revelations will be so many. The **GOD PRESENT**, **I** put in **THE FATHER'S TALK** is to show you that **I MYSELF THE SUPREME WORD OF THE UNIVERSE, AM THE FATHER'S TALK** (**GOD PRESENT**) Lecture Revelations. If you believe the contents of any piece of publication that carries **THE FATHER'S TALK (GOD PRESENT)** Lecture Revelations that testifies about **THE EVERLASTING GOSPEL, THE EVERLASTING WORDS OF GOD, THE SUPREME WORD OF THE FATHER GOD** that has come to reconstruct the world, then you are blessed. By believing this testimony you are okay and **I** mean totally okay!

Even, if you die, **I** can return you to the earth immediately to witness this **WORD**. **I** can do anything at all.

When you talk about miracles happening again then you should know that this is the only miracle that can happen. There is no miracle again to occur. The **TOTAL POTENCY** of **THE FATHER GOD** is behind **THE FATHER'S TALK (GOD PRESENT)** Lecture Revelations.

THE FATHER'S TALK (GOD PRESENT) information is to replace all negative information and energy on earth. **THE FATHER'S TALK (GOD PRESENT)** information has come to stay in three capacities in the **spirit**, the **soul** and the **physical**. THIS IS **THE SUPREME WORD OF THE UNIVERSE**.

In the name of Our Lord Jesus Christ
In the blood of Our Lord Jesus Christ
Now and forever more, *Amen*

THANK YOU FATHER

Contents

The Universal Supreme Invitation
                                        05- 06

Preface   07-19

Chapter One   *21-81*
The Supreme celebration

Chapter Two   *83-152*
The bylove of Word

Chapter Three   *153-200*
Every Reason

Chapter Four   *201-214*
The Voice The Creator

Chapter Five   *215-259*
The Inspirational Writers

THE SUPREME CELEBRATION

Chapter One

THE UNIVERSAL SUPREME WORD CELEBRATIONS SEASON

FATHER'STALK
(GOD PRESENT)

Date: AB/OA/OH (The twelfth day of the first month of the FATHER (year) two thousand and eight)

In the name of Our Lord Jesus the Christ,
In the blood of Our Lord Jesus the Christ,
Now and forever, more, *Amien*

THE UNIVERSAL SUPREME WORD CELEBRATIONS SEASON

> **THE WORD IS THE MAKER, THE FATHER GOD, THE CREATOR OF THE UNIVERSE.**

It pleases **ME THE FATHER GOD THE CREATOR OF THE UNIVERSE** to bring this Lecture Revelation tilted: **THE WORD IS THE MAKER, THE SUPREME WORD SEASON: THE UNIVERSAL SUPREME APPRECIATION SEASON CELEBRATION TO THE FATHER GOD THE CREATOR OF THE UNIVERSE.**

A: INTRODUCTION

I promised that after revealing the lectures titled **THE MANUAL OF THE SPOKEN WORD, THE MANUAL OF LIFE** and **THE INVESTMENT WITH GOD, I** would bring this lecture as a special revelation about the **SUPREME SEASON CELEBRATION. I** have brought this lecture to support HRM King Solomon David Jesse **ETE** for his innovative **GOODWILL**. For the first time in history, **I** have witnessed in spirit that since the creation, apart from Abel, someone has been celebrating **THE**

WORD SEASON. I have never heard it before. If there is anybody anywhere, that has kept a day, a week or a season aside as the official celebration for the **WORD**, the phenomenon called **THE SPOKEN WORD**, it is likely to be negative or have a negative motive, because, if anyone has done this in a **POSITIVE** mode without attachment of any evil, **I** would have noticed it in **MY** record. **I** have nothing to do with negativism and evil. **MY DIVINE SELF** is **THE HOLY SPIRIT** therefore anything that you do in the truthful form with **THE HOLY SPIRIT** records in **ME** directly. Because of Abel was the first **APPRECIATOR** it has pleased **GOD** that **I** have brought HRM King Solomon **ETTEH** of **BROTHERHOOD OF THE CROSS** and **STAR**. **I** have inspired him to establish the original **APPRECIATION** season for his **MAKER**, his **FATHER**, his **GOD**, the **SPOKEN WORD**, and the **WORD** is the **MAKER**. And since he has brought the original spirit and template to do this, **I** have to come out today to give him this record that **I** have kept for him and for the entire universe. **THE GREAT APPRECIATION SEASON** is for **THE ALMIGHTY FATHER GOD** your **CREATOR it** is via **THE WORD** and now **I** have given the everlasting promotional title as **THE SUPREME WORD SEASON CELEBRATION TO THE FATHER GOD ALMIGHTY, THE CREATOR OF THE UNIVERSE**. This is the title that **I** have given. Open you mind, correct you spirit, your feeling your emotion and accept this **WORD** about this wonderful innovation heart, try to re-arrange your mind, your nature and your destiny, because this is to prove whether you are for **GOD** or for evil. All the children of **GOD** on earth who believe in their **CREATOR** and want to **APPRECIATE** their **FATHER GOD** must pass through this **SEASON** as the entrance as the only one entrance by which you can **APPRECIATE THE FATHER** officially in a general reason. It is the **OFFICIAL SEASON,** however having given this instruction, wherever that human being finds his or herself is the kingdom of **GOD.** This **APPRECIATION** is not only for human **GOD**, it is for all human beings including human animals, human birds and human fish but human **GOD** offspring is the chief **APPRECIATOR** of today's lecture. If you go through most **THE FATHER'S TALK**, you will see in the record that **I** have revealed who Abel was and that he reincarnated as the King of Israel King Solomon officially the first time, however there are many transits of Abel. Abel stands for the **POSITIVE** son of Adam therefore all **POSITIVE** sons of Adam are actually reincarnated transit of Abeles. And all **POSITIVE** fathers are **POSITIVE** reincarnated Adams therefore, that is what is called **TRANSIT INCARNATIONS** and that are when you come to prepare your root before you actually come. In many ways, you have to be your own forerunner. Just as your thought thinks well before you speak and you speak before you act that the same way that **I THE FATHER** being the same spirit and **I THE FATHER** is the same **WORD** and **I THE FATHER** is also a human therefore, **I AM** complete and that is why you see **ME** bring this revelation. All **POSITIVE** human being would be so happy to come across this **FATHER'S TALK** because it comes straight from the mind of **GOD**, it is not from occultism and not from the intellect of the world, it is straight from **THE FATHER GOD** as **FATHER TALK (GOD PRESENT)**.

B: **IN THE BEGINNING WAS THE WORD**

Everybody sings this statement **IN THE BEGINNING WAS THE WORD AND THE WORD WAS WITH GOD and THE WORD IS GOD** but what have you done to prove this. It is the absolute **TRUTH** that in the beginning was **THE WORD** but where is the beginning? The beginning only starts from the physical creation but when you go into spirit, there is nothing like the beginning. The spirit is round and that is the meaning of **O**, the first **O** and it is round therefore when it circles you, you are included and everything that it circles is included and that is Brotherhood in spirit. **HE IS THE SPIRIT, HE IS THE FATHER** means that **I AM** revealing **MYSELF** because if your father does not give you the truth of his origin, it would be very difficult to know where you belong. If you check, what is happening in the world now and lot of human beings do not know their root. So many White and Black people do not know their roots in terms of where they actually eminent from. That is why a lot of them say that they are from space, some say they are from mosquito. Some say that they are from flies and others give different versions of where they came from because no one has given them the actual history of their root of origin of where they came from however you will now know your origin from this lecture. Today the origin of all human beings would be revealed in this lecture. **I AM** your **ORIGIN** and if you read the lecture titled the '*SOURCE AND DESTINATION*' then you would know that **I AM your ORIGIN**. What is the meaning of **ORIGIN**? **ORIGIN** means **HE IS THE SPIRIT**. And what is the meaning of **SPIRIT, HE IS THE SPIRIT, HE IS THE FATHER. I AM** revealing to you that **HE IS THE SPIRIT, HE IS THE FATHER** is a phenomenon that has no beginning and no ending and cannot be heard, touched and seen but **THAT SPIRIT** has become seen-able, heard and touched. Because it becomes possible to see anything that you can hear and when you can hear, it becomes possible to touch. However, if you cannot hear or see how will you touch it? Now **I AM** revealing **MYSELF** from **SPIRIT** to **SOUL** and from **SOUL** to **PHYSICAL REALITY** as **REAL, REALSO** and **AMISO** and that is

SPIRIT, SOUL, and **HUMAN**. The middle manager and the middle controller of all these things is **GOD**, the **SPOKEN WORD**. If you read the most recent lecture that **I** have revealed titled **'ALMIGHTY FATHER GOD, GOD AND GOD THE FATHER'** you will have more understanding about this. Some people would still be confused and ask whether **GOD** is three. **I AM** revealing **MYSELF** in three dimensions so that you may be better enlightened. You cannot hear, see, or touch **ME** as **SPIRIT** however because **I AM** hearing you, seeing and touching you, **I** transformed **MYSELF** to be in the **SOUL FORM** which is the **SOUND** to produce a meaningful **WORD** as the soul of the **SPIRIT** because of **LOVE** for **MY** creation. **A SPIRIT life in the WORD and because of that, the WORD is GOD.** The **WORD** makes **HIMSELF** seen after **I** have made **MYSELF** heard through the **WORD**. From this basis, it means that **I** have made **MYSELF** to be seen from being unheard and that is an **OBJECT SOUL** system and nature. **I AM** the **SOUL** and from the **SOUL, I** made **MYSELF** touchable in the human form. You should know your origin from henceforth, now that **I** have revealed **MYSELF** in this way. **I THE SPIRIT** manifests to be heard then, **I THE SPIRIT WORD, HEARD** manifests to be **SEEN** as an **OBJECT SOUL** without which, it would not be possible for you to touch. Since time immemorial, you have been seeing the sun but have you ever touched it? Also, have you ever touched the sky? There are so many things that you can see as shadows and objects but it is impossible to touch them. However, through **LOVE, I** have made **MYSELF TOUCHABLE** so that you can feel the physical form in order that you may feel at home and your mind can be at rest. Every touchable thing is **THE FATHER GOD**. **I THE FATHER GOD** is a **SPIRIT** but **I** transferred **MYSELF** to be **HEARD** as the **SOUND**, the **SPOKEN WORD** and then **I** transferred **MYSELF** from the **SPOKEN WORD** which is a **SEEN OBJECT** into a **TOUCHABLE** form as a human being and all other creatures and living organisms. This is why when **I** was on earth as **OUR LORD JESUS CHRIST**, **I** said, 'in **BEGINNING** was the **WORD** and through the **WORD**, everything that was made was and without the **WORD**, nothing that was made was made'. It means that without the **WORD** there are no physical manifests of anything. This is why today's, lecture is to direct every living soul to **APPRECIATE** their **MAKER**, the **SPOKEN WORD** in the divine way. Many people have been doing many things with the **WORD** but they have never honoured the **WORD** and **APPRECIATED THE WORD** but this is the revelation to direct you **APPRECIATE** your **MAKER, THE SPOKEN WORD**.

C: **THE SPIRIT LIVES IN THE WORD**

I, AM THE FATHER GOD THE CREATOR OF THE UNIVERSE, and I AM the **SAME SPIRIT** that is talking now. That means that **THE SPIRIT** is **LIFE** as the **LIGHT** of **LIFE** in the human heart which is unseen but you can hear that **SPIRIT** when it becomes the **SPOKEN WORD** which is wonderful! Is it not a wonderful thing that you do not see something but you can hear it? You can hear the thunder when it sounds in thundering modes but you will never see it. Who has ever seen a thunder? That is how, **I** bring **MYSELF** from **THE SPIRIT** to the **SOUND** by hatching **MYSELF** from **THE SPIRIT** to make a **SOUND** and from that, it becomes a meaningful **WORD. MY** thought is **MY SPIRIT** and **MY** voice is **MY WORD** as the **SOUL** and then **I** manifest an **OBJECT** through **MY MIND**. I create things in **SPIRIT** and give them **OBJECT-SOULS** before they come to manifest physically via the

PRONOUNCEMENT of THE WORD and that is why the **WORD** is **GOD** and that is what you should worship as **GOD**. This why people worship many things as God because what they worship is attached to the **WORD** as there is an instruction on how they should worship and that is how you can worship those things as a God. Many people from India have talismans and Egyptians have mould things to worship. **I** know what everybody is doing. They use gold and other metals and attach an instruction to it and then people buy it and worship it as talismans. It is all rubbish because there is nothing inside it. Why don't you attach to and worship the **REAL THING**. All the people that have rings and believe in the ring as a talisman and all those that believe in moulded images are all stupid because they have baby spirits in their nature and they are all second hand people as agents of elementary spirits. If you are an original human being, who through the reading or hearing from this lecture you come to understand that you have access to **THE FATHER GOD** and represent **GOD** because the **WORD** lives in you and you can speak, even as a small child, then you would not worship mere non living things that cannot even speak! Do you see why **I** say that you are stupid? People should worship you because when you worship a man you worship the **WORD** that is inside man. As such if the man speaks **POSITIVELY**, and represents **GOD** well as the **LIKENESS** of **GOD** then you are worshiping a true **GOD**. A true **GOD** is in man. The true **GOD** is not in a talisman neither is it in the wood, or moulded cement, a block or a tree or in all the things that you are worshiping. The actual true **GOD** lives inside man as the **SPOKEN WORD**. And when a man has **WISDOM** and speaks, his utterance is **GOD WORD**. **I AM** using man that **I** created to be touchable to talk through as **I AM** talking now. This means that **I AM** talking through **MYSELF** as **HUMAN** that **I** have made touchable as **MY**

HUMAN- SELF. However, the **WORD** is hear-able but if you do not hear the **WORD**, I exist as **UNHEARD-ABLE, UNSEEN-ABLE** and **UNTOUCHABLE** but you can see **ME** in **HUMAN**. And that is why if you offend any human being, do not forget that you have offended the **SPOKEN WORD** in that person. This why anyone that is involved in killing can never ever be forgiven because you have abused **THE HOLY SPIRIT**. Do you not know that the worse sin that a person can commit is to destroy life? No creature should destroy another creature not even the life of an ant, or any creeping thing. All the four living creatures as fish in all natures of fish, bird in all natures of bird, animals in all natures of animals and human beings in all natures either translated humans from other creatures or a real human should not be destroyed. If you abuse any of the aforementioned **LIFE**, you are going to stand for a particular judgement because **LIFE** is **ME THE FATHER GOD** and **LIFE** is the

WORD and that is why if you abuse **LIFE**, you will come back to commit suicide and that means that the **LIFE** that you have taken would be found in your hand. When a woman conceives for seventy two hours, that is three days and three nights, she should not abort, because when you abort, you are a murderer and have blood on your hands. It is only the original Abel who is now HRM King Solomon **ETTEH** that **I** have revealed a special code to on how to appeal for the nature to forgive anyone the sin of abortion because he was the first man that was killed. You should now be aware that there are secrets in things because if **I** do not reveal this to man, how will you know these things.

This **FATHER'S TALK (GOD PRESENT)** is the **LIGHT** of the world because the reason that when **I** came as **OUR LORD JESUS CHRIST I** said that **I AM THE LIGHT OF THE WORLD** is that if **I DO** not speak the mind of **THE**

SPIRIT you will not know. It is only the **WORD** that can tell you the mind of **THE SPIRIT**. People think a lot of things but since they do not speak, you will not know what their planning, so that you will know their mind? Sometimes when they speak, they divide the thought and tell you the one that they want you to hear and burry what they do not want you to hear in their mind. The deepest thing as the greatest thing on this earth is the **THOUGHT** of every human being. The most secret phenomenon on earth is the **THOUGHT** of human beings. The next one is the **WORD** of every human being but after that, the **EVENT** is a very simple thing. And this why **I THE FATHER GOD** is the **CAUSE**, the **EFFECT** and the **MATTER** of everything as such **I** judge according to the **CAUSE, EFFECT** and the **MATTER**, not just the **MATTER**. When you see something is happening physically, you do not know the cause of that thing, therefore you cannot just take action on what you see alone.

If you are **POSITIVE**, join in the reading of **THE FATHER'S TALK** through the School of the Higher Self Brotherhood Mastership by upgrading yourself through **THE FATHER'S TALK (GOD PRESENT)**. King Solomon Spiritual Library would unfold a lot of things for human beings. **THE SPIRIT** lives in **THE WORD** and you are now aware that **I THE FATHER GOD** lives in the **WORD**. This lecture does not need to be too lengthy because is it very plain and easy to understand. It is as easy as **ABC** and also simple because **GOD** is **SIMPLE**.

From the **SPIRIT** to the **SOUL** and from the **SOUL** to physical manifestation means that, **I THE SPIRIT** manifest as the **WORD** and the **WORD** manifest everything that you can see including human beings and lives in inside them. From this basis, the most secret phenomenal occurrence that every person should respect is the **THOUGHT** and after that, the next phenomenon is the **WORD** before a **HUMAN BEING**.

D: A GOOD WORD MEANS GOD

Whenever you want to know if someone is a child of **GOD**, you should assess their **WORD** because the fruit that human beings bear on earth is the **WORD**. If you want to know whether that person is **POSITIVE** as a true child of **GOD**, listen to their **WORD** because no matter how anyone may pretend and hide, it cannot last forever. One faithful day, the person would reveal him or herself. If he or she is **POSITIVE**, they would not forget themselves because it is the indwelling spirit that takes capacity of their life that would vibrate and make an utterance as a **WORD** which is **THE FATHER GOD** as **THE SPIRIT** that lives in that person. And because this is the **POSITIVE** side of **THE FATHER,** he or she would speak the **WORD** of **GOD** all the time, as a **GOOD WORD** that represents **GOOD** things which develop from **GOOD** ideas. From the **GOOD** idea, he or she would find every possible means to bring that **GOOD** idea into **WORD** as you are hearing now, the reason why the true children of **GOD**, the **POSITIVE** ones would believe that HRM King Solomon is the original Abel and also the original King Solomon is through this **WORD**. Forget about his physical outfit, rather go through all of **THE FATHER'S TALK** and you will know that it comes from an ENLIGHTENED **MIND**, the soul of **MYSELF** dwelling in him which is what forces out this **WORD**. If you give this **WORD** to the people that are not correct, they would not be able to read, even if you copyright the reading and give it to them; they would not be able to read, not to talk of how they can speak this **WORD** out. Tell an evil man that worships idols that he should kneel down and say my idol is dead whether he will pronounce that? He will not pronounce it. An idol worshiper would never say that his or her idol is dead. Tell a witch or a wizard, a talisman holder, or someone that is involved in the occult and has killed human beings that all the people that are involved in rituals and sacrificing of blood would die and see whether he or she would say it. They would not because they would be afraid. Tell the people that are involved in witchcraft to say that they would become mad and confess openly to the public in the hearing of people whether they would say it? Have you ever seen someone that farts in the public place and agrees that he or she is the one that farted when people say that he or she farted? The person would say it was not them because they do not want disgrace. Who on earth is able to confess openly that they are sinners however the truthful person is the one that bears the truthful fruit. It is said that, 'by their fruit ye shall know them'.

I AM bringing all these lectures and doing everything to demarcate the children of prediction from the children of **GOD**. If you are a **POSITIVE** child of **GOD**, then forget about whether you attend a church or a mosque or any other place of worship, forget about your religious affiliation, and forget about the colour of your skin as a black or a white person or your levels of education. All you need be, is a human being that speaks or uses the **WORD** other ways to use this opportunity to acknowledge your **CREATOR**, your **MAKER** and your **GOD** through this directive. Forget about all the celebrations that you have been celebrating because many human beings celebrate their birthdays but do you know the meaning of your birthday? How do you manage to have a birthday to celebrate but you do not celebrate the **WORD SEASON. I** want to open everyone's eyes, because people complain about having problems in their life and in their family saying that they do everything GOOD expected from them but **EVERYTHING OF EVERYTHING IS THE WORD.** Do you acknowledge the **WORD? A GOOD WORD** means **GOD** because every **GOOD THING** means

GOD, but do you acknowledges **GOD** in your life? This lecture alone can save your soul if you accept and practice it and **I** mean it. If through this lecture, from this day, you acknowledge **ME** in your life by **THINKING GOOD, SPEAKING GOOD** which will materialise **GOOD** event as **GOD** then **I** will save your soul. Who told you that man is not **GOD**? Even a **GOOD** tree is **GOD**. A **GOOD** animal is **GOD**. Some animals are vegetarians and they have never killed another animal therefore, they are **GOD**. Do you think that the Whale that swallowed Jonah and vomited him would have done so if it was not **GOD**? Have you ever seen a bad lion that catches an animal that does not devout and eat it? Have you ever seen a prostitute that catches a man and does not fornicate with that man? Have you ever seen a fornicator that catches a woman and does not fornicate with that woman? Have you ever seen a rat that catches a fish in a basket and refuses to touch that fish unless it is a vegetarian therefore the Whale that swallowed Jonah him alive was a vegetarian and **GOD**. And this is how you know what the Whale is, by its fruit. If you see anyone that does not speak evil and does not hate people and practices **LOVE, KINDNESS, PEACE, MERCY** is **RIGHTEOUS,** has **HUMILITY** and is pure in heart then that person is **GOD**. If **GOD** lives in you then you are **GOD** and your presence means **GOD PRESENT**. However, if you have hatred, tell lies and are crafty and hate people, having jealousy, envy, strife, arrogance, pomposity and segregation, then you are Satan. Where you see envy and strife, all evil things live there. When you are envious and jealous of someone, you can never look the person in the eye or like that person, because you think that, the person is better than you or is more powerful and why should that person be glorified more than you should? Is this not what happens when other children of **GOD** are jealous about King Solomon **ETE** as Cain was jealous about Abel? This means that all those who are jealous of King Solomon came from the tribe of Cain the great vampire. And all those who are not jealous came out from the tribe of Abel, The Origin of Human God. **I** brought King Solomon back in the kingdom of **GOD** so that if you are jealous about him, then you are Cain and **I** would mark x on your forehead so that you continue to be jealous and at the end of the day, you will destroy your soul because you shall pay for it. If you are not jealous and have **LOVE, HUMILITY PEACE** and are **HAPPY** with someone, for whatever that person is as it is you because you are part of that person then you would have a share in what that happen has. If you are **GOOD**, you are part of **GOOD**. Do you think that gold will be annoyed to see gold? For instance, if you take a small gold and throw it inside of a container with big gold's, the small gold would take glory with the big gold because when people look in the container, they would see gold and that is it. When you see a group of human beings walking together in a group when some are small as young children and others are big as adults do you not see the beauty? And nobody says get up you are a small child or you are man or a woman because of **LOVE**. When people honour a president, a king or queen his or her servant or assistant would share in that glory. Do you not understand these things? If you are a child of **GOD** and speak a **GOOD WORD** and the **HOLY SPIRIT** dwells in you then **GOD** is in you because as a result of THINKING **GOOD, you** speak **GOOD WORDS** which proves that the spirit of **GOD** is in you and makes your presence, **GOD PRESENT** because you are the house of **GOD**. From this basis, you speak as **GOD**, and when you walk, you walk as **GOD**. Whoever honours you, honour **GOD**, not you as a man but the **GOD** in you and then you become an **APPRECIATOR**. You should now **APPRECIATE** the **WORD** that **MADE** you **GOD** and acknowledged you because if you acknowledge the **WORD** the **WORD** will acknowledged you and **I THE FATHER GOD** will acknowledge everything and that is how the glory of **GOD** will manifest. **GOOD WORD** means **GOD**. Wherever, the **GOOD THOUGHT**, the **GOOD MIND** and the **GOOD WORD** emerges, there you will see the alter of **GOD** because the tabernacle of **GOD** is with man and the **WORD** of **GOD** is in man. That is why the kingdom of **GOD** is in man, the city of **GOD** is man, the nation of **GOD** is man, and the universe of **GOD** is man. Everything that you can talk about **GOD** is man because **GOD** lives in **WORD** and the **WORD** lives in man and **THE SPIRIT** lives in the **WORD** and the **WORD** manifests as man and in man. What do you use to govern? Is it not **THE WORD**? It is not your physical presence alone but when you speak the **WORD** all your subjects understand and take the instruction. Even if you are physically present as a King and sit down in your throne but do not speak, it does not mean anything. Carry anything like talisman, or idols and anything that you can think off but without the **SPOKEN WORD**, it has no meaning. It is the **INSTRUCTION** as the **WORD** that attached to that thing that makes people value it. The value of everything is the **WORD** attached to it. When you read, the lecture titled *'THE VALUE'* then you will understand more about this. All occultism masters and all evil doers as wicked people in any gathering whether in the dream or physically or within any gathering without the **WORD** being used then it does not mean anything. Use this opportunity to acknowledge yourself as a **POSITIVE** person of **GOD** and speak the **GOOD WORD** to prove that **GOD** dwells in you. When you speak evil as the negative **WORD**, **GOD** is not dwelling in you. When you **THINK WELL** and **SPEAK WELL** and have **LOVE, JOY, PEACE, MERCY, KINDNESS, RIGHTEOUSNESS, HARMONY**, then more **GOOD WORDS** would bear the

POSITIVE fruit in you. From this basis when you start to speak the events of all these things will start to manifest and that is how the world would change for **GOOD**.

E: THE WORD IS THE CREATOR

After having all the said **GOOD** things in your heart and you are able to think well, through **THE SPIRIT** because the **HOLY SPIRIT** lives in you then, you will create well. You have to understand the meaning of the difference between **PACKAGING** and **CONTENT**. The actual product can be a liquid but how would you handle the liquid until the final user uses it. The liquid needs a container and that is why you have to buy a container and put the liquid inside the container but that is not the end of the matter. After that, you will need to describe the content. The description that you put on the container would give the directive on how to use the product with the name of the **PRODUCT**, the

MAKER, and the **CONTENTS** and that is the enlightenment about the product. However, the product itself is the liquid that is inside the container and the container itself is just the package. Within these analyses, **I THE FATHER GOD** is the **PRODUCT** but **I** only survive in ideas. The idea about the product is the formula itself and that is unseen, unheard, and untouchable because it is the **SILENT FORM**. When the formula is completed then there are all sorts of condiments to add, such as salt, pepper, and species and finally when you add up all the ideas as a component into one then, it becomes the actual product which is a packaged soup that you would take and drink.

When you finish producing the above as an idea form in your **THOUGHT,** then you will now synchronize it with an inscription which is the writing as the **WORD** by a lecture or seminar where you can teach people to use your formula to produce a nice soup that is either African or English that people would enjoy. After this, they would use the idea and cook the soup and the physical liquid of soup is now ready for consumption but what is the container that holds the soup before people would drink in their mouth. It is at this stage in the system of **THE FATHER GOD** that man comes into the matter. The **SPOKEN WORD** has finished the work after the **THOUGHT** has given the formula. However, the thought that gave the formula is in the shadow form as **SOULS** and the **SOUL** has brought it out through the **SPOKEN WORD** to become soup. This is the point where you need a container to put the contents and that is why **I** created man as the harbour of the content and the name of the man that describes the content is the **WORD** that makes everyone to be enlightened about the product therefore everything among the product is one. When you take a product called '*African soup nu.1*', will you say that the packaging is not a part of it or is it the name that is not a part of it or is it the actual soup that is not a part of it. When you consume the soup that you have, it does not mean that the soup is finished because the soup is still in another package elsewhere therefore the name continues to exist and that is how you use the name to find that soup. Wherever, you see the package you will know that, that is the soup. And as long as the formula exists, the soup will remain forever this why the **WISDOM** of **GOD** is the energy of everything. For this reason, **I THE FATHER GOD** has come to reveal everything about, and to all creation for whom **THE WORD** is their **CREATOR**. When you speak a **GOOD WORD** thereby creating a **GOOD** event then you represent **THE FATHER GOD THE CREATOR OF THE UNIVERSE**. And the **WORD** that lives in you will not leave you comfortless because since you are representing well, it would also be well comfortable with you.

F: THE WORD IS IN EVERY PERSON

Will you argue that the **WORD** is not in every person? Even the damp as one that cannot speak uses the **WORD**. It does not mean that they do not have **THOUGHTS** unless there has been an accident in the foetus. When everything is well then even a child that is inside the womb is thinking. It takes GB (seventy two hours) for a foetus to start thinking inside your womb however the action from the thought of the foetus is through the mother. Do you know that there are some spirits that after seventy two hours of conception they start to direct you? They can even direct the two parents, the mother and father. What you want to eat will change, how you behave will change because of that foetus. The way that you behave will change, your health will change and everything about you will change because of the foetus that has come into you as a visitor. An errand man, a messenger or some sort of spirit is visiting but you are carrying him or her inside your womb as a portion of another world that is different from the one that you are breathing in. As a result, your character, your instinct and everything around you will change as the mother that carries the child. And when you as the mother changes, it would affect the father of the child who lives with you. Suppose the child that is coming is child from the **HOLY SPIRIT** who does not eat meat and fish and is a vegetarian, then after seventy hours of conception, when the mother sees meat and fish she will vomit. Do you know why pregnant women always vomit? What they eat before they became pregnant and what they eat when they are pregnant is not in conjunction with the child, and then he or she would drain it all out to make space for him or herself. When this spirit that is the **WORD** is in you, your character will change and you can be extra happy or you can be very moody. If the child wants to grow with fruits and vegetables then that is what the mother would like to eat. Anything that the child wants is what the mother will feel like eating. The mother will go out of her way to get the particular food that the child wants. This means that something inside you is directing therefore, you cannot live according to your dictation again. You live according to the partial dictation of the child that you have conceived. And because you cannot stand fish and meat, it would affect all the children in the house and also your husband as the father of the child. Since you cannot stand fish and meat and you do not cook it, then your household would also not eat it. And this is why anyone that has the **HOLY SPIRIT** in them would surely have a changed life for **GOOD**. The **WORD** is in everyman therefore if the **WORD** is **GOOD** from a **GOOD THOUGHT** then it is from the **HOLY SPIRIT**. The **POSITIVE SPIRIT** lives in you because you have invited the **POSITIVE** spirit through your **FAITH** because everything works according to **BELIEVE** and **FAITH**. **FAITH** is the magnet that **GOD** gives to humans as a **FREEWILL** heart. When you have **FAITH** in something and **BELIEVE** it then will attract that thing that you believe to yourself. From this basis if you believe this **WORD** and start to gel **FAITH** and join the universal group of oneness to celebrate the **WORD SEASON** and if you do this for three years, you will see a one wonderful change in your life. Even if you celebrate for only one season, from the day that you accept this instruction and this order and recognize yourself as the house of the **POSITIVE SPOKEN WORD** and deny all negativism and all evil minds you are blessed. Deny jealousy, deny strife, deny arrogance, deny pomposity and deny segregation and division. And also deny a wicked heart because that is the spirit of witchcraft. Also, deny all talisman, and deny hanging things thinking that it would help you rather it would give you bad dreams and link you to have bad company in the evil spirit therefore if you deny all these things and **BELIEVE** that the

WORD is you then you are saved. Do you not know that in you, there is a spoken **WORD** and there is a **SPIRIT** that lives inside you? If a baby that has been conceive as a foetus can act in the mothers womb, then how much more your life when the **WORD** lives in you? Do you not have a **THOUGHT**? If you change all the negative **THOUGHT** to **POSITIVE THOUGHT** and it grows with that, it grows well with you then **THE FATHER GOD** will take glory then you will see that the **WORD** is in every human being. And since the **WORD** is in every person as the **LIGHT** of **LIFE** shining it conquers all darkness, then you can think well and speak well then **GOOD** event will materialise through you. You can bear **ME** a witness that this **WORD** is **TRUE** because you can **SPEAK** and when you **SPEAK**, ninety- five percent of your **WORD** is carried out. From your children to all your people pay attention to your **WORD**. If you say, bring this, they will bring, stand here and they would stand and sit down here and they sit down. Everybody uses the **WORD**. In the work place, everybody uses the **WORD** to communicate with each other. The master uses the **WORD** to instruct and the servant also replies back with the **WORD** by saying 'yes I would do that' and all that is **THE LIGHT OF THE WORD, GOD HIMSELF** as the **CREATOR OF HEAVEN AND EARTH**, and the **IN-DWELLER** in the human body. The tabernacle of **GOD** is man and **GOD HIMSELF** dwells in you but you have not known all this time. Tell **ME**, if someone gives you something to use to help yourself, as having some sort of power, where is the power from. Is it not the **WORD**? The person that gives you this thing **BELIEVES** this thing and since he or she **BELIEVES** this thing, it gels more power in him therefore anything that he or she tells you to do when you do it, it works for you because you **BELIEVE** and that is how the **POWER** works. For this reason if you **BELIEVE** this **WORD** today then you will become a store room of **POWER** and a master and director via the **WORD**. The **WORD** is equally available to every soul and it is only when you do not tap it or your capacity is low then the current of the **WORD** becomes low in you but the **WORD ITSELF** is **GOD** and that means **EQUALITY** for every man. This lecture will have many parts but this is part one.

G: **JOIN THE FIRST APPRECIATOR**

This is the order now from **THE FATHER GOD ALMIGHTY** to all human souls as human being, fish, bird, animal and all creation on earth to join the first **CHIEF APPRECIATOR**, to **APPRECIATE GOD THE FATHER ALMIGHTY** on earth. And who was the first **APPRECIATOR**? It was senior brother elder Abel and you can add any **POSITIVE** title that you wish. After Adam, the next **POSITIVE** man on earth is Abel and that is why **I** sent Abel officially as a King to Israel to inherit his father Adams's throne. However, Cain was there and wanted to take over the throne. And who was Cain? It was Absalom and he was the person that killed Abel and now he wants to kill Abel again but it did not work because if you hate someone, **I** will make that person to rule over you so that you will become a slave to that person. Every soul that hates another person will be in the same position. From the day that you are jealous and hate someone, **I** will put you under that person as a slave so that it would be painful to you. And that is why **I** say that those who humble themselves would be raise, but those who raise themselves would be debased. From the day that you hate someone and speak evil about them, and assassinate their character, indirectly trying to kill that person with all your jealousy and strife and that person does not retaliate, then **I THE FATHER GOD** will take all your **GOOD** deed and give to that person and upgrade that person the more. And **I** would do this because you have subdued that person therefore **I** will raise him or her and subdue you but in actuality it is not **ME** that subdued you, rather you subdued yourself because of evil your practice. When Cain killed Abel because of jealousy through the spirit of vampire, Satan, Lucifer as the serpent in him, **I** subdued Cain just as **I** subdue his indwelling sprit that was Lucifer to crawl on the ground as the serpent.

King Solomon succeeds because **I THE FATHER GOD** is within him. At the same time when his **FATHER** came the second time as **OUR LORD JESUS THE CHRIST**, the same spirit came to fight him and who was that? It was Judas Iscariot and at that time, he was still a family member as he was in the case of King Solomon. **I** will have a special lecture for this but **I AM** mentioning it here because **THE WORD** comprises of every **POSITIVE** thing. **I** give you the background family history so that you will know yourself and know how things manage to be the way that they are. Judas Iscariot betrayed **CHRIST** and that is indirectly killing **CHRIST** but if you want to go to the root of the matter, he was actually the person that killed **CHRIST** through that betrayal. **I** have sent three angels to go ahead of anyone that hates someone. From the moment that you conceive an evil thought about someone, you will be arrested. The **GREAT CHANGE** will take effect in you unless it was in the person's destiny that you should successfully do what you are doing to that person for a purpose. If not so, you cannot do anything to that person and that is why Absalom could not kill King Solomon, even though King Solomon ruled from when he was a child because right from his birth, he was ordained a King in the throne of his father. The same thing will continue to happen till tomorrow, therefore if you like, join this great movement with the **GREAT APPRECIATOR** who is **ABEL** the **INCARNATE KING SOLOMON DAVID JESSE OF ISRAEL AND NOW**

INCARNATE HRM KING SOLOMON DAVID JESSE ETTEH in Ikwo-Okwo, Akwa Ibom State, Nigeria. Join him by celebrating the **GREAT APPRECIATION SEASON, THE WORD SEASON**. He has established **THE WORD SEASON** by keeping ten days aside for that celebration for the first time. He started since nineteen eighty nine and **I** have been taking it easy, but last year in two thousand and seven, he made it **AO** (ten) days of celebration and **I HAVE APPROVED THAT FOR ETERNITY!** And he also established the **TRINITY WEEK**. The **WORD SEASON** is for all **CREATION** because anybody that **THINKS** and **SPEAKS** or **WRITES** must join him in celebrating **THE WORD SEASON**. This would be by observing the seven days for the **SEVEN SPIRITS OF GOD CREATION** and three days for the **SPIRIT, SOUL** and **PHYSICAL HUMAN** and that makes **TEN** days **SEASON** of **CELEBRATION**

OF THE WORD SUPREME SEASON CEREMONY.

Joining the **GREAT MAN** of **APPRECIATION** to **APPRECIATE THE FATHER GOD and that WOULD** bring a **GREAT BLESSING** to the entire world. It is because of the **APPRECIATION** ceremony conducted by Abel for **ME** that brought the birth of **CHRIST** because **I** came to the world to save him. And that is why if you celebrate the **WORD SEASON** then you will see that the **WORD** would support you. You know that you **SPEAK** the **WORD** for your children to listen so celebrate this **SEASON** then all your children would listen to you. Celebrate this **SEASON**, as **POSITIVE** human being and all **POSITIVISM** will support you. **I** do not refer to negative people because negative people have a package of negativism but of you celebrate the **WORD SEASON** then the package can change. The **WORD** can change your destiny for **GOOD**, the

WORD can give you **GOOD** luck, and indeed the **WORD** can do anything for you therefore, do not ask questions and saying ' since King Solomon **ETTEH** is the **CHIEF APPRECIATOR**, what **GOOD** thing did he have, what has he given to the **FATHER** GOD'. My dear think well about it, because for **ME, THE FATHER GOD THE CREATOR OF THE UNIVERSE** to talk through him and bring all these archive records and all this **WISDOM** and this enlightenment that would save the entire world and change you as the one that you are hearing now, it means that he is well, well blessed. And he has unlimited wealth.. In fact, he has **UNLIMITED COMPREHENSIVE MEMORY OF GOD**. What is money compared to that? For generations of generations you will read **THE MANUAL OF LIFE, THE MANUAL OF THE SPOKEN WORD, INVESTMENT WITH GOD** and this **SUPREME SEASON'S APPRECIATION** then you will know that nobody else can have this

WIDE- ANGLE OF GOD to be **NEARER** to **THE FATHER GOD** and through this, you would be **NEARER TO THE FATHER GOD**. Through the **WIDENESS** of **GOD** and **INCLUDED**, **I** have drawn a cycle and **INCLUDED** everybody that believes this **WORD** and then **I** draw you **NEARER** to **MYSELF**. This means that you are **FREE** from witchcraft spirit which is the vampire spirit of Cain and you are **FREE** from the spirit of Queen Sheba who **I** have changed through the bosom of King Solomon and that means that you are **FREE** from the Queendom spirits and all negativism. You **FREE** from occultist, you are **FREE** from all those who worship Idols and or carry talisman because since **THE LORD IS THAT SPIRIT**, where **THE SPIRIT OF THE LORD IS, THERE IS LIBERTY**. From this basis, you can see that this lecture alone is worth more than Brillion's of money or any carnal thing that you can think off in this world. And if you donate trillions as **I** donate **MY PHYSICAL**

LIFE to die for man, it is not enough. **I** have now decoded the channel of **APPRECIATION** to **GOD ALMIGHTY**. And **I** would give instruction on how the **APPRECIATION** should be directs to **THE FATHER GOD**, in the name and the blood of **OUR LORD JESUS CHRIST** *Amein*.

If you want to join the **CHIEF APPRECIATOR** to **APPRECIATE GOD**, then this is the only acceptable way. Before you **APPRECIATE GOD** openly deny all use of talisman, deny all idol worshiping, deny all negative practices that you have joined and any acknowledgement that you give to any elementary gods and spirits. If you do not do that and you **APPRECIATE THE FATHER GOD** then **I** will not take it because it is like giving the appreciation of Cain and this is the **TRUTH**, and it is also as putting a dish in a dirty plate to serve it to **ME**. Anyone that is not **PURE** in heart and does not have **MERCY** and you do not think well, and speak well yet says that they **APPRECIATE GOD** is a liar and **I** would not take such a gift. You may think that you can donate in the church after you have killed or prostituted yourself then bring the money to **GOD** and **GOD** will forgive you. It is a lie because that is not **ME**, the **GOD** to whom you refer. **I** know the evil people would say that it is not **GOD** that speaks but judge for yourself in your mind as to whether you are truthful? You order people to donate things to **GOD** and they are prostitutes and killers and wicked people who have joined secret societies because you are part of them but you are preaching and calling the name of **GOD**. You use these situations to make money for yourself and then you say that you are worshiping **GOD**. Which **GOD** are you worshiping? You are rather worshiping your stomach. **GOD** needs a **PURE HEART** and **RIGHTEOUSNESS** because if you give something to **GOD,** but you are not **GOOD** then **GOD** does not want it. **GOOD** means **GOOD** but you are not **GOOD** and you donate for **GOD** how does that work? Abraham gave ten percent of his dividends to **GOD** from killing people and taking their things but **I** did not take it. He gave ten percent for recognition of **GOD** but when he had Isaac, **I** demanded Isaac for **APPRECIATION**. And since he offered Isaac, it means that he gave **ME** his heart which is what **I** was demanding. **I** did not want him to kill Isaac, it was Satan that wanted him to kill Isaac so that there would be no tribe of **GOD** on earth but **I** changed that to an **APPRECIATIVE HEART**. **I** do not want sacrifice. The way you **APPRECIATE ME** is to have **LOVE**, to have **PEACE** and to **BELIEVE** in **ME, THE FATHER GOD**. It is not because **I** say you should join HRM King Solomon so you bring money to trap him money because you are a wicked person or a prostitute that wants to go closer to him to fornicate with him. Or because you are an evil man, you gang up with political aims and other aims to get blessing from him but that would not work. First of all, you must **LOVE** and **FORGIVE ONE ANOTHER** and **BELIEVE** in this **WORD** and **PROMOTE** this **WORD** as the **POSITIVE WORD**. Be **HONEST**, be **PEACEFUL**, be **KIND**, be **MERCIFUL** be **TRUST WORTHY** and **BELIEVE** and **STAND** with **THE TRUTH** and **LOVE EVERYBODY** then, **I THE FATHER GOD** will build you as **MY** container and live in you. From this stage, **THE GLORY OF GOD** will manifest because **I** will take anything that you give **ME**. And if after you repent, you bring your wealth to build a universal shrine for **ME**, through King Solomon, **I** will also take it. Without this, forget about it. Do not remember what happened when King David wanted to build a temple for **GOD**? **I** said no and told him that rather his son, Solomon would build because his hands were soiled with blood. If **I** can do that to **MYSELF** in David, who are you to donate for **GOD** with an impure and an unholy heart? You build Bethels, Cathedrals and build this and that, but you go about duping people, joining secret societies and disgracing **THE FATHER GOD** in you and then you come and donate for **ME. I** do not want such donations. You say that you serve **GOD**, but you go about to defame people's characters, telling lies, hating people and doing all sorts of things that does not suit children of **GOD,** and then you call yourself a child of **GOD**, a man of **GOD** and a servant of **GOD**, then you are a deceiver. You are Cain, you are Absalom, and you are also Judas Iscariot. If you want to be Peter or James and you want to take the **POSITIVE SPIRIT** of Abel then **LOVE ONE ANOTHER** and be humble then in the presence of **HIS HOLINESS** on earth, the **KING** of **KINGS** and the **LORD** of **LORDS**, you will see **MY** face in the **POSITIVE WAY**.

CONCLUSION A: **BROTHER ABEL IS BACK ON EARTH WITH HIS FATHER ADAM**

I AM now announcing openly through this lecture something which **I** have spoken of many times already. **I** revealed **MY DEITY** to the harbinger of **GOD**, Professor Assassu Inyang Ibom. He is the official spirit soul that **I** keep aside as a prophet to reveal **MYSELF** whenever **I AM** here on earth. He was Isaiah, he was also John the Baptist and in this generation, he is Professor Assassu Inyang Ibom. He has revealed that the witness of **GOD** as the servant of **GOD** brother Abel is back on earth with his father Adam, The **KING** of **KINGS** and The **LORD** of **LORDS OLUMBA OLUMBA OBU**. If you do not believe this, it is your cup of tea and up to you, because the **TRUTH** does not worry when lies rise it head, **TRUTH** stands forever and it is unchangeable. If this **WORD** is true and **I** have come as the **HOLY SPIRIT OF TRUTH, LEADER OLUMBA OLUMBA OBU** and **I** live in King Solomon David Jesse **ETE** to reveal all these things to humankind, and you refuse to accept, then the cause, the effect and the matter would find you out for a **GREAT CHANGE** to take place in you.

CONCLUSION B: ALL POSITIVE HUMANS MUST FOLLOW THEM

I have registered and testified in the **SPIRIT OF TRUTH** that this is a **TRUE** revelation and all **POSITIVE** human beings should follow it to **APPRECIATE THE HOLY SPIRIT OF TRUTH**. For this reason, you must spread this news and encourage people to believe **THE FATHER GOD, THE SPOKEN WORD**, first in your heart then follow with practical signs of **HUMILITY, LOVE, PEACE, ONENESS, MERCY, KINDNESS** and all other **GOOD** things. From hence, you should **THINK WELL, SPEAK WELL** so that you can **DO WELL** in all aspects of life. Whether you are a president, a king, a queen, prime minister, a preacher, a man, a woman, a child, or any other position that you hold does not matter in so far as you are a human being and the **WORD** lives in you and you **SPEAK** the **WORD**, then, you must join this **GREAT MOVEMENT**. To bring every human being on earth to acknowledge the **WORD** as his or her **CREATOR** is a task that must be done, because with this, the whole world would come together.

FOR UNITY AND THE WORLD PEACE

There is no more division and segregation. Everybody in the world would celebrate the **SUPREME WORD SEASON** in their homes, in their communities, in their local government areas, in the states, nations and world wide, be you Christians or Muslims. You must find out when this **SEASON** is from HRM KING Solomon. All governments, all presidents and heads of all countries should declare a public holiday for all their citizens during this period. Every human being that manifest from each of the spirit of **GOD**, that is from Adam to **CHRIST (Sunday to Saturday)** represent the seven spirits of **GOD**. Each of the days represents the house of **GOD** as the **SOUL CREATIONS** in the world of paradise and the three days is for **THE FATHER, THE SON** and **THE HOLY SPIRIT** and that is the spirit, the soul and the **WORD** that lives in you and that is why it is a **TEN DAY SEASON CELEBRATION**. It is the **SUPREME CELEBRATION** on earth. When you do this all tributes goes to the **SPOKEN WORD** which is **GOD THE FATHER** in manifestation. During the celebration of the **SEASON**, make sure that you take care of orphans, the destitute, and the old and poor people and do as much **POSITIVE** charity as you can. Do not go to war with anyone and do not fight. Allow people to be in **PEACE** by forgiving **ONE ANOTHER** and that means that you should release innocent people from prison, and not take people to court. This means that you **THINK WELL, SPEAK WELL, HEAR WELL, SEE WELL** and that would lead you to **DO WELL**. These are the first fruits that everybody must bear during this **SEASON** and it should take place every time in your life all years for eternity. Since HRM King Solomon ETE celebrates this **SEASON** from the first of the tenth month to the tenth, **I** have sign that period until he changes it. **I** accept his and all those who will join him to show **APPRECIATION** for eternity, and the following is how **I** want the proceeds shared when it comes to physical donations in cash and kind. Thirty (CO–30%) percents, as **TRINITY** should go to The **KING** of **KINGS** and the **LORD** of **LORDS, HIS HOLINESS OLUMBA OLUMBA OBU,** THE UNIVERSAL SHRINE representing **THE FATHER GOD** on earth, the final Adam. Thirty- (CO–30%) percent should go to **OUC – THE SUPREME UNIVERSAL CHARITY ACCOUNT,** the purse that every human being on earth has a hand in and it is used for taking care of the less privileged and all peoples in the whole world. Another twenty (BO-20%) percent should go towards the management of **THE FATHER'S TALK (GOD PRESENT)** through HIS ROYAL MAJESTY KING SOLOMON DAVID JESSE ETE, and that is King Solomon Spiritual Library at THE WORD CITY **(THE SUPREME WORD MANAGEMENT ACCOUNT).** And the ten (AO-10%) percents should go to the government of the nation as tax. The balance of Ten (AO-10%) percent should go for organizers of the season to use it in ministering the **THE SUPREME WORD SEASON** to continue. For the portion of thirty (CO-30%) percent that is going to the OUC – THE SUPREME UNIVERSAL CHARITY ACCOUNT, ten (AO-10%) percent should go to Muslims OUC – Charity Account, and ten (AO-10%) percent to Christians OUC – Charity Account, this is THE SUPREME WORD WILL to mark the unity between Muslims

<u>and Christians in the manner of Honouring Our Great Father Abraham, the father of all nations. The balance of ten (AO-10%) percent goes to general brethren of the land. The Centre Management of OUC – THE SUPREME UNIVERSAL CHARITY can take some (%) percentage from each of the three internal account for administrations. By the time that this **FATHER'S TALK** would be prove read, any sprinter of **word** would be corrected.</u> **I MYSELF** always come and correct everything before assimilation to the world.

CONCLUSION C: **THE TRUTH HAS COME**

Now that the **TRUTH** has come to manifest **ITSELF**, all these things are **GOOD** and everyone should adhere to it. Use **LOVE** to check yourself, because there is no law, apart from **LOVE YE ONE ANOTHER**. This Lecture Revelation would be accompanied with the information goes with all **THE FATHER'S TALK** titled '***WITH LOVE***' so that everybody would be **FREE** to choose. It is the agreement and acceptance directive of **THE FATHER'S (TALK GOD PRESENT)** so that everyone should use his or her **FREEWILL** to believe or not to believe. However, you use the **SPOKEN WORD** in you kitchen, living room, your bedroom, your work place, and you expect people to believe you therefore think well about whether it is **GOOD** for you not to believe this **WORD** when you know that the **WORD** is everything. If you do not believe and pay the royalty for the **WORD**, by believing and celebrating the **WORD SEASON** then if the **WORD** ceases out from you, then do not blame the **WORD** rather blame yourself because that is when you shall see what you will become. It is only a dead man that cannot join this celebration, but if you are a living breathing human being then you must join **THE SUPREME WORD SEASON FOR THE SUPREME UNIVERSAL**

APPRECIATION SEASON CELEBRATION TO THE FATHER GOD THE CREATOR OF THE UNIVERSE, now and forevermore, *Amien*.

Let **MY PEACE** and **BLESSINGS** abide and remain with the entire creation especially human being now and forever, more, *Amien*.
In the name of Our Lord Jesus the Christ,
In the blood of Our Lord Jesus the Christ,
Now and forever, more, *Amien*.

ENYE ODUDU ABASI ME, OOO ZIM ZIM ZIM ASASU, POSITIVE, POSITIVE, POSITIVE

THANK YOU FATHER

Chapter Two

THE UNIVERSAL SUPREME WORD SEASON CELEBRATION (GOD PRESENT)

THE BYLOVE OF WORD

FATHER'S TALK
(GOD PRESENT)

Christ Our Lord, Twenty-third Simon Canaanite, FATHER, Two Thousand and Eight (BC/OB/BOOH) Saturday, Twenty-third February, Year Two Thousand and Eight (23/02/2008)

**In the Name of Our Lord Jesus Christ
In the Blood of Our Lord Jesus Christ
Now and forever more**

THE UNIVERSAL SUPREME WORD SEASON CELEBRATION [GOD PRESENT]

THE BYLOVE OF WORD

Today it pleases **ME, THE FATHER GOD THE CREATOR OF THE UNIVERSE** to give this Lecture Revelation titled - **THE UNIVERSAL**

SUPREME WORD SEASON CELEBRATION – (GOD PRESENT), an official *'by love'* (laws) for *THE UNIVERSAL SUPREME WORD SEASON CELEBRATION* program to recognize and appreciate **THE FATHER GOD THE CREATOR OF THE UNIVERSE.**

INTRODUCTION:

AIM AND OBJECTIVE

The aim and objective of this program is to **RECOGNIZE AND SHOW APPRECIATION TO OUR FATHER GOD THE CREATOR OF THE UNIVERSE, THE SUPREME WORD OF THE UNIVERSE.**

The Aim and Objective is to make every creation especially human beings of all types – those who speak, those who think, those who hear the word to join His Royal

Majesty King Solomon David Jesse ETE, to celebrate and appreciate The **WORD**. You should understand that you are not appreciating HRM King Solomon David Jesse ETE. Rather you are only joining Him for the celebration and appreciation of **THE SUPREME WORD OF THE UNIVERSE.** This is what He has been doing. **I** have talked about this singular action of King Solomon ETE for a long time and severally. Nonetheless, nobody should say that it is King Solomon that planned this. It is **I THE FATHER GOD ALMIGHTY, THE SUPREME WORD** at this fullness of time for this to be done, as it is done in Heaven.

The Aim and Objective of this particular **FATHER'S TALK** (GOD PRESENT) is to give awareness and also present the mechanisms that is, *'the by- Love'* (laws) and the directives for the celebration. In this regard, whosoever that asked questions should be handed this

FATHER'S TALK for the person to read. This is official introductory information manual for the program of recognizing and appreciating **THE FATHER GOD, THE CREATOR OF THE UNIVERSE AS THE UNIVERSAL SUPREME WORD ALMIGHTY.**

The Aim and Objective is so that **I, THE FATHER GOD** will use the exercise to forgive mankind and restore mankind back to the original state that mankind was with **THE FATHER GOD** in the Garden of Eden.

The Aim and Objective is for mankind to link back with **THE FATHER GOD.** Read the Lecture Revelation titled *'The Universal Lineage'* to know. So, when you link back with **THE FATHER GOD** then will you realise that **THE FATHER GOD** is ALL and ALL that lives in you. And that **HE** is Everywhere, Here and There.

The Aim and Objective of this program is to identify the original positive children of God that is, those who came directly from

THE FATHER GOD and not from the vampire, which are the virus infected ones. The vampire children are those that the evil virus affected their nature. **I** have to separate them. Just like during the time of harvest, you harvest your produce and separate the good crops from the bad ones. The office situation is another analogy. In the office for instance, at the end of the financial year the bad accounts are separated from the good ones. Then the bad ones are sorted in whatever manner the company will like to handles and treat that account. Similarly, the farmer checks their crops and stock and some of the crops that did not grow or germinate well or are damaged are thrown away. So during the harvest period, the good crops are separated from the bad ones.

For the human race, this is inspection time. **I AM** going to give a Lecture Revelation called 'The **Universal Supreme Inspector**'.

The Aim and Objective of this program therefore, is now clear to every soul. There should be no iota of confusion and doubt regarding this program. The intents and purposes are laid out in such a simple manner so as not to confuse anyone. Therefore, this does not warrant asking any questions – the irrelevant and or unnecessary ones.

The Aim and Objective is to reveal the importance of The **WORD** **HIMSELF** as **THE CREATOR OF THE UNIVERSE,** The Maker and also your life as you are living. Without The **WORD** you cannot live. This is also to show you, how to show gratitude to The **WORD** as well as to appreciate your life and also your maker, The **WORD**. The **WORD** has never charge you, because you cannot pay for your life. Nonetheless, this celebration is to let you know, since you do not know including everybody else, matter of fact all creations, but human beings in particular that there is need to celebrate and appreciate The **WORD**. The entire humanity and indeed all creations never thought of appreciating The **WORD**, when they are supposed to appreciate The **WORD** who keeps them alive, they are rather misused the **WORD**. Without The **WORD** you cannot do anything. You cannot be. Since you did not know, now you will know and have known that you must be obliged to the **WORD**.

If you question this that means you are really, really revealing yourself as a bad and very negative human being. I cannot see the reason anybody should question about this activity, by asking questions such as - why and for what reasons this should be done. If you really argue over this Divine Holy motivated and innovation mind, then there is something very, very wrong with you, just like Lucifer, the senior Evil, the Leader of Rebellious groups, I hope you are not one of those.

I want to make it clear that this arrangement is not for the benefit of any particular human being. Every human being that breathes air must appreciate The Word inside them and so participate in this program. That is the reason the motto is *"ALL WORD CELEBRANTS"* – 'EVERY HUMAN BEING IS A CELEBRANT OF THIS UNIVERSAL PROGRAM'.

Who and what are you celebrating? You are celebrating THE WORD that lives in you, which is **THE LIFE** in you. This is also to show respect to The **WORD** and to believe The **WORD**. **HE** is your **FATHER GOD,** your Creator and everything to you. The whole world, all creations, mankind and entire universe should now know that this is the time to believe, to recognize, to acknowledge, to accept and to obey **THE FATHER GOD ALMIGHTY,** less will see what **I THE SUPREME WORD** will do to you with that oxymoron spirit of Lucifer in you. This culminates the *Aim and Objective* of the introduction part of this Lecture Revelation.

This particular **FATHER'S TALK** is *An Official Introductory Manual of Information for the Program to Recognize and Appreciate* **THE FATHER GOD THE CREATOR OF THE UNIVERSE.**
The title of the program is – **THE UNIVERSAL SUPREME WORD**

SEASON CELEBRATION. In Heaven, on earth and in all planets, it is The **WORD** that keeps all of them. Where The **WORD** is not, life is not there. Even where there is no life, there is The **WORD**. Therefore, even in the Hades, this **WORD** Season celebration must take place. This **SUPREME WORD SEASON CELEBRATION** is now forever established.

I use His Royal Majesty King Solomon David Jesse ETE to initiate this program. **THE FATHER'S WORD – THE FATHER GOD** in him is the Inspirational Head. King Solomon did this in the Garden of Eden as Abel. Now **I** have brought him back to re-establish it here on earth. You must therefore, join him for the celebration of **THE SUPREME WORD**.

B: **THE PAST PRESENT AND FUTURE WORD**

***The Past, Present and Future* WORD** – we are now going into the accounts. From the time of creation to the present time and the future for eternity, what will be? Ask yourself what is going to be. What was, what is and what is going to be? The WORD that was, The WORD is and The WORD to be. There is no way The WORD can be removed from anything. The WORD is the leader to every manifest. **HE** precedes any physical manifestation. Everything must pass through The WORD first by thinking, followed by speaking and then the doing takes effect. For the action to occur The WORD must design and approve everything, before the action takes effect. Therefore, The WORD is the *Past*; The WORD is the *Present* and The WORD is the *Future*.

If you are dead before now, you must celebrate **The WORD Season** wherever you are that is, wherever your soul is. If you have opportunity to celebrate that means God has chosen you. That is, you are short-listed.

All the people in the whole world that accept this program are short-listed. When you believe this program and join it and appreciate well then **I, THE WORD - THE SUPREME SPIRIT** that lives in you will short-list you. **I** live in every soul and motivate the action of The **WORD** in your heart, in your mouth and by hearing. **I, THE SUPREME SPIRIT – HE IS THE SPIRIT** motivates all actions in you.

The **Supreme WORD** is as a result of **MY SPIRIT – MY SUPEME SPIRIT** in you. So, if you do not recognise The **WORD** and honour The **WORD** worship The **WORD** and celebrate The **WORD**, you will never know what

THE FATHER GOD is. That is why **I** said that nobody is able to know **THE FATHER GOD,** unless you know The **SON**. Also, nobody can see **THE FATHER GOD** unless you pass through The **SON** who is The **WORD**. This is The **SON** of God. This is God **HIMSELF.** This is **MY Soul. THE FATHER GOD'S** SPIRIT manifested The **SPOKEN WORD** and this **WORD** lives in every soul. Therefore, as per living **I AM** indirectly in everything created by The **WORD**.

I do not create and then abandon **MY** creation. The **WORD** lives in every living organism and every living creature. That is the *past, present and future*. Those who came to the world before now must equally appreciate The **WORD**. Even if you do not believe in reincarnation, you have been here before. Nonetheless, today, you are here in the world and you are hearing this word. If you are not yet born when you are born you will hear this word. The program covers past, *present and the future*, since The WORD will never die.

The WORD is called *"ODUWEM" and "UWEM"* and because of that everything must be included in this program.

ODUWEM is the Soul part of **The WORD**, while *UWEM* is the Spiritual part of **The WORD**. The two System form The SUPREME WORD of the Universe in your system. That is the reason that you can be alive. Even when you die, you come back to be alive because no human being dies. The soul in you and the spirit in you never die.

Therefore, The WORD covers the *past, the present and the future*.

C: **UNIVERSAL**

What is the meaning of *Universal*? Since The **WORD** stands for the past, present and the future, what does *universal* stands for?

Universal means generality – all and all. It covers all space. It covers all planets.

Universal means Heaven that is, spirit and soul and the Hades and here on earth. In short, it covers Everywhere, Here and There. EVERYWHERE, HERE AND THERE - some humans do not understand the phenomenon called EVERYWHERE, HERE and THERE.

EVERYWHERE, HERE and THERE constitute the living places of **THE FATHER GOD THE CREATOR OF THE UNIVERSE.**

I AM EVERYWHERE. That is The Spirit.

I AM THERE. That is The Soul.

I AM HERE. That is the physical manifestation.

THE FATHER GOD is living in those phenomenal places in the three capacities.

That is the meaning of The Universe. Therefore, this program is *universal*. There is nowhere you can run to from hearing the knocking on the door for you to participate in this program of celebration of The **WORD**.
MY SPIRIT will be knocking in your spirit, in your soul, in your heart, knocking in your past, knocking in your present, and knocking in your future. WHEREVER YOU ARE **I** MUST RECEIVE THE FRUIT OF **MY** LABOUR as THE CREATOR OF THE UNIVERSE, AND THE MAKER OF ALL THINGS "**BROTHERHOOD**".
Nobody respects those who serve God via the **WORD**, the Preacher and the Teacher. Look at the cunning of evil, Preachers and Teachers are the leader of the world, because there are the servants of the **WORD**, but now who or which government of this whole world recognized them, rather Satan make the so cal big people, even government sponsors

evil programmes and wars here and there. The worst thing about the negative spirit of Satan and what she did was giving negative response to God's ordinance not to appreciate The **WORD**. People follow Satan to make that worst mistake and humanity still makes that mistake in this world by refusing to acknowledge the fact that everything on earth is managed and directed by The **WORD**.

Thinking, speaking and hearing are the processes to go through, before any action takes place. **I** will give proper relevant explanation in this Lecture Revelation, so that you are not left with half knowledge of what you should know. For sure **I** know that there is none who knows the truth, and then the truth refuses to set the person free. Since the whole world is not free, today you are going to be free by this truth. Free in spirit, free in soul and free in your physical present if you obey this *universal* instruction.

Let **ME** inform you very well of this. If you do this *Universal* Program, you are free. If you do not do the program you are an everlasting debtor. As a result you will never feel fine, because your conscience will forever blame you, just as Lucifer with bad conscience till today because of disobedience.

To be free, you must in the first instance, accept this program with an overwhelming joy. Be very happy! Be in a good mood! Show joyfulness! Be extremely happy about this program! **THE *UNIVERSAL* SUPREME WORD SEASON CELEBRATION!** Wonderful! Wonderful thing! Wonderful inspiration! Wonderful innovation! The greatest innovation on earth! The greatest idea on earth for mankind!

The whole world including, all governments, all heads of organizations etcetera - all those who love **THE FATHER GOD,** who love The **WORD** and who use The **WORD** must give

HRM King Solomon David Jesse Etteh Award for initiating this program.

I, THE FATHER GOD has given him award! **I** have started giving him awards as THE BUILDER OF THE FUTURE, THE BUILDER OF THE KINGDOM OF GOD and THE SUPREME **WORD** SENIOR APPRECIATOR. Therefore, every human being on earth must thank **THE FATHER GOD** in him for initiating this program and other wonderful programs that nobody ever initiated. For that reason, it is a must that every human being on earth that thinks, that speaks, that hears and takes action of any sort through The **WORD** must join this program. If you don't do, you must do. That is the meaning of *UNIVERSAL*.

I AM decoding and expatiate in each **WORD**, which is in the title of this celebration program - **THE *UNIVERSAL* SUPREME WORD SEASON CELEBRATION. I AM** deliberating on each of the **WORDS**. **I** have now finished deliberating on *UNIVERSAL*. The next one is SUPREME.

D: **SUPREME**

What is the meaning of *SUPREME*? It is an English **WORD**. The reason **I** use English Language for now to give all **THE FATHER'S TALK** especially this "By Love" (laws), is because the last visit of King Solomon Etteh on earth was in the United Kingdom. He was the first King – King James. **I** have said this time without number that King Solomon David ETE was King James of England. If you do not believe that means you do not believe and it does not matter. However, **I** emphatically state again that His Royal Majesty King Solomon David Jesse Etteh now in Nigeria – Africa, in his last visit on earth was King James of the United Kingdom. He came as King James to specifically establish and edit an approved version of the positive Holy Bible, An Authorise Version.

The United Kingdom was the missionary base and for that reason **I** established him to spread the **WORD** of God and to help all the scattered children of Israel in the whole world, which was the meaning and the original idea of United Kingdom. The seat of dragon also got established there, so **I** moved the potency of the **WORD** to United of America and the dragon followed.

Wherever **I** went to establish **MYSELF** as the **WORD** CITY, the dragon carried its seed to establish there too. However, now it will no longer work for the dragon, because **I, THE FATHER GOD ALMIGHTY THE CREATOR OF THE UNIVERSE** have established **MY THRONE OFFICIALLY IN AFRICA,** and also the **WORD** CITY. That is where everything was started in the first place.

Africa is THE SOURCE and THE DESTINATION. So, **I** have now connected the whole world back to where everything started. He who laughs last laughs the best.

The whole world now knows that all riches, all hopes, matter of fact all their lives and everything is in Africa. It is their Father's land.

Africa is the Land of Peace; the land of Milk; the Land of Honey; the Land of Respect and the Land in which everything started. Where you have the SOURCE that is where you should have the DESTINATION the three RINGS CIRCLES "OOO". So, **The *Supreme WORD*** has come and the **Supreme Celebration** has commenced.

THE WORD is THE *SUPREME*.
THE SPIRIT is THE *SUPREME*.
I AM THE *SUPREME* – THE *SUPREME* FATHER, THE *SUPREME* WORD, AND THE *SUPREME* CREATOR. Call everything about **THE**

FATHER GOD *Supreme*. Universal is the *Supreme*. **I AM** all the information in this **FATHER'S TALK. I, The WORD, AM** explaining **MYSELF**. The **WORD** is an endless phenomenon. It is infinity. It is the '**Cyclical Encyclopaedia**'. There is no beginning and no end of The **WORD**. The **WORD** goes in and comes back out. It is round, round and round. It is endless. It is the time – the second and all. It is everything. Therefore, The **WORD** is *Supreme*.

There is nothing on earth that can be assigned with The *Supreme*, other than THE SPOKEN **WORD**. This is so because The *Supreme* Spirit is unheard-able, unseen-able and untouchable until **I** made **MYSELF** heard-able through The **WORD**. So, The **WORD** is the first *Supreme*. Upon all this, nobody has recognized The **WORD**, generation upon generations. Nobody recognizes The **WORD**; nobody honours The **WORD**; nobody respects The **WORD** but you use The **WORD** to do all sorts of things, both positive and negative. So you can now see that The **WORD** is the King of Kings and the Lord of Lords. It is the *Supreme* Administrator - the *Supreme* Manager, *Supreme* teacher. The **WORD** is *Supreme* of everything physically here on earth.

The first thing man can hear - the sound is The **WORD**. Through The **WORD** I become touchable from heard-able and seen-able. Without The **WORD** you cannot see **ME.** Without The **WORD** you cannot touch **ME.** It is The **WORD** therefore that brought **MY SELF** to seen-able and touchable. For that reason **I** must respect **MYSELF** in The **WORD**; I must recognize **MYSELF** and celebrate **MYSELF** in The **WORD** before any other thing.

I THE FATHER GOD, which is THE SPIRIT unheard-able, unseen-able and untouchable - without any knowledge that is, awareness of THE SPIRIT then, it was The **WORD** - **MYSELF** being **THE *SUPREME* WORD** brought **MYSELF** with awareness into physical reality.

I AM *The Real* in spirit and **The WORD** is *The REALSO. REALSO* manifest *AMISO.* Alleluia! This is *Supreme – Supreme* Wisdom! There is no other wisdom that is greater than this. That is the meaning of *Supreme*.

Let **ME** emphasize on the *Supreme*. **DO NOT CALL ANYTHING *SUPREME*, EXCEPT THE WORD, EXCEPT THE FATHER GOD, EXCEPT GOD THE FATHER.**

THE FATHER GOD is the only *SUPREME*. This **WORD** program is the *Supreme* Program. Other programs on earth must be under this program. The reason is simply addressing this simple ideology of how and where you could possibly undertake any program or do any thing without The **WORD**. You must therefore, appreciate everything positive to do with The **WORD** in all gathering, individually, severally and otherwise. Without that you will be called to account for your negative action.

Also anything you do with your thought, especially when you want the thought to be fruitful that is, to be brought into physical reality, you must call this program to mind. If you want to make statement about your thought in the bid to bring the **WORDS** into life you must remember this program.

When you show appreciation you would not ask any question regarding what **I** said before now that –

THE WEALTH, THE BLESSING, THE WISDOM, **I** GIVE TO HIS ROYAL MAJESTY KING SOLOMON **I** WILL NOT GIVE TO ANYBODY AND **I** WILL NEVER GIVE TO ANYONE. EVEN NOW AND AFTER NOW HE REMAINS **MY** PROPERTY.

HRM King Solomon David Jesse ETE is **MY** bedroom. He is **MY** Privacy. He is **MY** Cold-room. He is **MY** Memory. That is the reason **I** said if you hate any human being on this earth, you are a wanted person, because you do not know who anybody is. Everything of **THE FATHER GOD** is buried in **WORD** in human; **WORD** is the totality of all creations as a package. Human being is a package where the spirit **WORD** can live and manipulate things.
All philosophers, all scientists, all honourable human beings in which The **WORD** lives inside of them know what **I AM** talking about, And they all will be

so happy to hear about this innovation. Any truthful person, any correct human being, the media and all will be so happy about this news. This wonderful *Supreme* News!

No matter what you do, if they are done through The **WORD**, whether singing, speaking and hearing and any other manner, use it to appreciate **The WORD**. In showing appreciation you must remember that **I AM THE FATHER GOD** through His Royal Majesty King Solomon David Jesse ETE of Ikot-Okwo, Akwa Ibom, Nigeria Africa, established this program.

I know some people are likely to be disgruntled and would grumble that everything Nigeria, another Nigerian man, Nigeria - Africa – black man. Yes! Where there is carcass there will be vultures! Don't you know that? Where there is smoke there is fire. Why should everything not be Africa? Why should everything not be Nigeria? You must know. Generations and generations must know why it is so. Check things well, check your mind – if you are spirit check in spirit. Check, check, check well about what is happening in Nigeria, Africa.

I AM directing the pointing arrow to where this **WORD** for the UNIVERSAL *SUPREME* **WORD** SEASON CELEBRATION came from. Where the arrow rests, **I** will break it into pieces unless the arrow is green, which stands for peace. You can then go there.

So, **THE *SUPREME* WORD OF THE UNIVERSE** is THE ONE that every living creature, spirit, soul and human must celebrate. Then **I** will use it as a mark to shortlist your soul that you appreciate **ME**. That is the first thing that **I** want from you humankind, HE AND SHE THE ALL **WORDS**.

E: **WORD**

Now we come to the central point of this Lecture Revelation of this program, which is **The *WORD* HIMSELF,** because the title is **THE UNIVERSAL SUPREME *WORD* CELEBRATION** and the point of focus is The *WORD*.

The next deliberation is **The *WORD*** and it fell on number **E** (five) – Five Star – the five points star. The letters *W O R D/ I K O* man – well, **I** will decode the letters later.

I will decode the letters of **The *WORD* – the meaning *WORD* or *I K O*** in another lecture. Though **I AM** using English language, they can be translated into many other languages, because all languages are one. The meaning of a *WORD* is the same thing in every language.

So, if you need to do anything worthwhile, present this in every language that man speaks. Make sure that you love **The WORD** if you want blessings. If you want your soul to be short-listed by **THE FATHER GOD** that you are on the positive side, make sure you interpret this program into all the languages of the whole world. That will be wonderful blessings for you.

Therefore, **I** want everybody to accept that what lives in your heart - what makes you a living soul – what quickens you is **The WORD**. The quickening spirit in you is **The WORD**. The Light of the world is **The WORD**. Without **The WORD** nothing will move in this world. Those who cannot speak can possibly write or speak with their hands and fingers. There is so many ways to speak **The WORD**. You can even speak **The WORD** with your eyes and your eyeballs. Therefore, all the people that use **The WORD** must appreciate **The** *WORD* in cash or kind and time. Use everything good to promote **The** *WORD*. Promote **The** *WORD* appropriately and truthful. You must believe this program.

When you mention these *WORDS* – **THE UNIVERSAL SUPREME** *WORD* **SEASON CELEBRATION** you must remember ***King Solomon Spiritual Library*** where this information came from. It then links you to **MY** physical presence on earth, The King of Kings and The Lord of Lords of the Universe. That is how the link is established in this program.

THE *WORD* is everything. This *WORD* – *WORD* is indescribable. It is unlimited phenomenon. This information is the best for this program. **I** do not need to give any other license.

From today, no human being should toy with **ME, THE** *WORD*. No human being should toy with this Supreme Program of celebrating **The *WORD*** . If you are a duper and if you are negative of any kind keep your evil tendencies with you and be far away from this program. Do not bring your negative actions to this program. If you do you will be sorry for your soul.

Nonetheless, if you are a bad person even if you are the worst person on earth, you can use this program to correct yourself. Join the program, think well, speak well and hear well regarding this program. If you do that, you may be forgiven. You could change for good.

People's opinion or impression of you is - this is the worst person or this is a prostitute and deserves punishment from God. But from the day you hear of this program and join it **I** will change you from your prostitution, and any evil way to good, just like **I** changed Rehab and Mary Magdalene as told in the Holy Bible.

People say of you - oh you are notorious killer; you've killed a lot of people - you hate people - you are wicked to people! But as you hear this program, you change and join this program. **I** will then change you, just as **I** changed Saul to become Paul and he became a righteous person. Any evil you commit whether armed robbery - any evil at all you do or have done, if you join this program **I** will change you and correct your instinct.

This program will aid to change over your instinct to good and so you recognize **THE FATHER GOD.** As you are a roam about spirit or roam about soul you have become evil. However, since you have come back home, as you join this program, you now know your destination by celebrating and appreciating **The** *WORD*. There is no amount of money, and there is no amount of time or anything you can give to equate with the benefit, value and the phenomenal standing of this program of **The** *WORD* **SEASON CELEBRATION.** There is even no degree of kindness you can show enough of or any kind of virtue you portray and demonstrate that is enough. There is nothing you can offer or does that would make **ME** say it is too big to appreciate **The WORD** with. Nevertheless, what **I** need from you first and foremost is to love one another, to be peaceful, practice righteousness, kindness, mercy and oneness. All governments of the world must practice equality. This is applicable to all human beings, all families - human beings of all sorts. Wherever you find yourself practice love - in the village, township, office, government, churches, anywhere, here and there, in the spirit, soul, physical and the heavens and on earth, the water – all planets.

What **I** want from all of you as regards showing appreciation to **The WORD** is to first love one another, stop wickedness, practice unity and peace, oneness and equality. Share all the amenities of this world in equal proportion to every inhabitant of the world, because they all manifested through **The WORD**. If you do not do this then it means you have signed to be enemy of **THE FATHER GOD** and you know what follows you. You cannot fight your life.

Nobody can fight his or her live. **THE FATHER GOD** is your life; **The WORD** is your life. So, if you are against this program, you are against your life and you cannot fight your life. That is direct judgement. **The WORD** is in you and **The WORD** you are celebrating is you yourself being the celebrant. Think about this.

When you hear this program, the next thing to do is to start telling people about it. When you start telling people and are happy about this then, **I** will link you to **MYSELF.** Then **I** will show you how the program will come about. As a result you will be a contributor on how to promote, how to arrange, how to sponsor and let in everybody.

When you sponsor this program you are helping souls. The **WORD** program is the most charitable program on earth that will help the entire mankind in the world. Everybody has equal share in the proceeds of this program, in spirit, soul and the physical. This program will help to make the whole world one in all aspects of life for instance, finance, trading, welfare, in the **WORD** and the rest of other things. As a matter of fact, this is the first program that **THE FATHER GOD ALMIGHTY** has established to bring everybody together. The program is also to show that we – the entire world are all one from the same **FATHER GOD – THE POSITIVE TRUE BROTHERHOOD**.

F: SEASON

The program is the celebration of **THE UNIVERSAL SUPREME WORD *SEASON*.** This is the point **I** want to declare this celebration to the whole world.

People would ask how this managed to be. Who or what gave the physical Initiator and Inspirational Head His Royal Majesty King Solomon **ETE** the audacity to do this? Who gave him this wisdom? You have not made any mistakes to ask these questions, because when you ask questions you know things. However, your questions must be positive and through positive mind.

If you ask this question through a positive mind that how did **THE UNIVERSAL SUPREME WORD *SEASON* CELEBRATION** come about. Then this is the answer:

From the time of old starting from Adam and Eve and their offspring, **I** needed to identify the children of God. These are those who believe that **THE FATHER GOD** is their creator. In so doing, they can use **ME – The WORD** well to manage the affairs of their lives individually, severally, collectively and generally in the whole universe.

So, **I** ordered that two children of Adam should appreciate their **FATHER GOD ALMIGHTY - The WORD** that lives in their Father Adam- also the same **WORD** that lives in them. Cain did not do it well. He grumbled about it, and was annoyed and was also jealous. Abel took good steps and offered a worthy sacrifice to **THE FATHER GOD.** Abel's sacrifice was not because he killed goat or ram or sheep or anything of the sort. It was the mind of appreciation. It was his mind of appreciation that **I** took.

You have to know that it is not you killing goat, cow or anything and drinking the choicest wine, champagne, beer and all the rest of them to celebrate that **I** want from humanity. It is your heart - the heart of celebration – the happiness. The oneness of taking in this information and the acceptance of this information is the first thing **I** will take from you.

Abel accepted the voice of God and he believed that it was good to respect honour and show appreciation to **THE FATHER GOD** who created them – to **The WORD** that lives in them. As a result **I** took that acceptance and the establishment of appreciation by Abel and regarded it very high. **I** then counted that action as righteousness to Abel.

When Abel Reincarnate and became King Solomon David Jesse of Israelite, though before that he had come and gone in many ways and many times **I** will not go into that now. As **I** was saying, when Abel came officially to inherit his father's throne, as King Solomon, the King of Israel, he did the same thing by building an outstanding temple for God. He showed extremely appreciating heart to **THE FATHER GOD** by demonstrating that the status of **THE FATHER GOD** should be as honoured as **THE ALMIGHTY FATHER GOD, HE IS THE SPIRIT WORD, and He** built a **SHRINE** to house **THE UNIVERSAL SUPREME WORD**.

Some would argue that it was his father David's program that the son Solomon did. Bear in mind that some people come to this world and destroy their father's program. Not every child that follows their father's footsteps, unless that child is your replica. What happened with Rehoboam? After Solomon, his child could not follow his footsteps and the program stopped. You see that? Nonetheless, **I** have brought back the program. Do not therefore ask unnecessary questions – what season, what **WORD**, what is this or that?

This *seasonal* celebration lasts for ten days. Seven days for all celebrants that is, **The WORD** that lives in you. Then three days are for the Spirit, Soul and Physical **WORD** Manifestation as **GOD THE FATHER** that is, The Trinity. Therefore, the three days marked out plus seven days total the ten days celebration for **GOD THE FATHER,** the Alpha and Omega Season. **THE WORD** *SEASON*

IS, ALPHA AND OMEGA *SEASON*. Alpha and Omega is, AO (Ten) – Ten Day celebration.

It would not matter whether any government gave holiday or not for the celebration. However, the governments that honour **The WORD** and use **The WORD** to rule if they are positive, if they want peace they should declare Ten Days' Holiday for **The WORD *SEASON*,** and take a positive active part in the programme.

During the period of celebration of **The Word *Season*** and through out the ten days duration there are required observations.
The season is not the time to drink alcohol.
It is not the time to fornicate.
It is not the time to go to war.
It is not the time to go out for witchcraft activities.
It is not the time to practice evil of any kind or any incantation and doing wickedness.

During this period you must single yourself out from any form of negativism. You must accept that **HE IS THE WORD** has short-listed you and stands by you to help you in everything you do with **The WORD** regarding how to honour and respect **HIS** ordinances.
I AM not giving you laws. Rather, **I AM** giving you love. These words mean love. They are not laws. Nonetheless, conscience will blame you when you refuse to act according to instructions.

During the period, declare yourself nice and so treat everybody nicely and be positive. Practice all manners of positivism. Sing songs, be prayerful, celebrate with everything good and show appreciation to God and with joy. Do good things. Anything you would like to do as part of the celebration let it be good and positive. Carry out charitable activities. Do good thing as much as you possible could. Help people, including your government under this umbrella and during the time. Do good things anywhere at any place and for everybody without discrimination, so that **I, THE FATHER GOD** will be happy with you and happy with the all humankind in whole world. Any government, any power, any human being that supports and promotes this program will be called blessed at all ages and for all times. So, THE *SEASON* is **THE UNIVERSAL SUPREME** *SEASON* **CELEBRATION.**

The *Season* means the period that is singularly kept aside for **THE FATHER GOD** - for **The WORD**. Everyone should note that this *Seasonal* **WORD** Celebration, King Solomon David Jesse ETE is the person that Holy Spirit uses to start it. Therefore, nobody should use the position they occupy and *'big man'* or presidency, seniority or philosophy or academia and academic attainment, any position or post, spirit or soul to rob shoulders with His Royal Majesty King Solomon David Jesse ETE. Respect The

Servant of **THE HIGHEST ALMIGHTY FATHER GOD.**

Respect him whom that God talks through. When you do that you are blessed. Your failure starts when you say, who that is! When you say that you fail instantly in your heart, when you fail in your heart then you fail everywhere. When you say that, that is when your failure starts. That is when your evil is revealed.

On the contrary, if you are happy and want to hear more and want to know more, you do not need to see King Solomon ETE for anything. All you need to do is to be happy with him. You should support him. Let your spirit support HRM King Solomon in this program. If you do that wherever you are **I AM** the **WORD** is in you and **The WORD** will bear you witness.

You do not need any physical person to bear you witness or keep record of your activities for you. You do not even need to worry about who would keep your records or who would keep records of your good deeds.

When you think well, speak well and hear well about this program **The WORD** will report you to **HIMSELF** and **The WORD** keep record for you. However, when you want to donate cash or in kind and otherwise or even time, then you can physically connect to the Central Celebration Program Office. Then everything is well with you. That is **THE UNIVERSAL SUPREME *SEASON* CELEBRATION.**

The period for the celebration is from the OA of OG to AO (First of the Seventh month to the tenth of the Seventh month). OA in the New World Counting is one, OG is seven and AO is ten, – OA – AO OF OG. The Seven month of the year is October, OA of AO to AO of AO (First of October to Tenth of October) every year for eternity is the period everybody is to celebrate **THE UNIVERSAL SUPREME WORD *SEASON* CELEBRATION.**

That is that. Whichever month is the Seventh month is the period for the celebration.

When the New World Calendar will take effect in the whole world, the period will be shifted to the OG (Seventh) month of the year. At present in the world, the AO month, which is the tenth month, is what you call October. That therefore, is the *SEASON* for the celebration. So, from the first of October to the tenth of October every year for eternity is **THE UNIVERSAL SUPREME WORD** *SEASON* **CELEBRATION.**

G: **CELEBRATION**

We land at number G, the seventh point of this program – *CELEBRATION.*

As you know **THE UNIVERSAL SUPREME WORD SEASON** *CELEBRATION* **– GOD PRESENT** is the title of this program. Now, the G is *celebration*. How do we *celebrate*?

What is the meaning of *celebration*? *Nam idara! Nam uyom! Kwo ikwo! Nek unek!* How do you do that? In the first instance:
You must love.
You must have peace.
You must be a peacemaker.
You must be kind and practice oneness.
You must be merciful.
You must possess Mercy and Love, righteousness, Kindness and Peace. Without all these things you will not be able to *celebrate* or partake in **THE UNIVERSAL SUPREME WORD SEASON *CELEBRATION*.** If you are not peacemaker for instance, Satan will use you to cause trouble and then you fail. If you do not have love, you will not be able to accept this program. You will ask lots of questions – who is this? Who is that?

Why is this and why is that? Lack of love makes people ask unnecessary questions. If you do not have love, you have jealousy and hatred.

Therefore, the reason you must have peace is so that the environment in which you are is sanitised for you to *celebrate* and receive your blessings. The reason you need to have love is so that you can accept and practice charity. Love one another during the *celebration* season.

Why do you need kindness? It is so that you can show kindness to all persons that **The WORD** dwells in. Those are your bothers and sisters. Do you know why everybody is your brother and sister? It is because the same **SPIRIT** - the same **WORD** that lives in you lives in them and that is **THE FATHER GOD.** What is the meaning of **FATHER?** It means the Rightful owner of everything.

If somebody can live in everybody that is your **FATHER** and that is your controller, just as your carnal father's blood is detects to know who really your father. Show **ME** anything that lives in everybody. It is only **The WORD** that lives in everybody. And this **WORD** owns the blood in you. This **WORD** owns the water in you. Without **The WORD** there is no water and no blood.

When a man died did you see evidence of good water and blood in him afterwards? When a woman died was there evidence of good water and blood in her? Water and blood can only be found in those who are alive as **The WORD** lives in them. **The WORD** is the owner of water and blood while **THE SPIRIT** owns **The WORD**. So, if you *celebrate* **The WORD**, you *celebrate* all. And you also *celebrate* man. That is the totality in meaning of loving one another.

When you *celebrate* The **WORD**, you will not have the heart to kill any human being because The **WORD** lives in human beings. Any human being you plan to kill has The **WORD** in them.

So, those who would not *celebrate* The **WORD** are the killers and the murderers as well as the wicked people. You would refuse to *celebrate* The **WORD** because you want to kill The **WORD**; you want to hate The **WORD**; you want to imprison The **WORD**; you want to be wicked to The **WORD** and everybody including yourself.

Therefore, if you refuse to accept this truth, you have already committed spiritual suicide, because when you refuse The **WORD** you refuse your life. Judge this **WORD** by yourself and your conscience whether it is true or not.

The *celebration* and the *celebrant* are both you. When you are *celebrating* **The WORD** directly and indirectly you are *celebrating* yourself, because **The WORD** lives inside you.

Without **The WORD** will you go to work?

Without **The WORD** will you farm?

Without **The WORD** will you go to the church?

Without **The WORD** will you sing in the church?

Without **The WORD** will you preach?

Without **The WORD** will you talk through the radio or the television? Therefore, all media including, television and radio broadcasting and the broadcasters, presenters, the tabloids, all forms of publishing and publications, IT and even the Internet…everywhere, here and there use **The WORD**. So, it behoves you who use **The WORD** to appreciate and *celebrate* The **WORD**. You can equally use this program to promote your own program. Everybody is affiliated to this program. All aspects of living and all lives endeavours, for instance, services, duties, labours, leisure - everything on earth is affiliated to this program.

This is the most powerful of all programs in the world. Bill Gate of Microsoft must respond positively to this program, because he is the co-chairman of this program in spirit. Bill Gate is the manifest of the angel called ***HESIGNSTIN*** as **I** revealed in the lecture **I** gave on Bill Gate of Microsoft. So, the indwelling self of Bill Gate is the angel called ***HESIGNSTIN.*** Word Processing City must be established at Ikot Okwo.

Bill Gate must sponsor this program. If he refused to sponsor this program, when **I** finished with him in this generation, next generation he will be the hater of good things and a loser. However, if he sponsors this program he stands to benefit. So, anyone that has access to this program should make sure he or she draws Bill Gate's attention to it.

Lots of people are doing so many charities both positive and political charity. None however, has done anything to recognize **THE SUPREME WORD OF THE UNIVERSE.** You must do it now! You ask - Where is this coming from? Who is the pioneer of this program? Somebody must be the head of something. **I THE FATHER GOD** passed through and dwells as God Present in His Royal Majesty King Solomon David Jesse ETE, **I AM** the ONE who have come to do this. This is one of the greatest revelations on earth.

Celebration and *Celebrant* – *Celebration* is the act of *celebrating* the *celebrant*, which is **The WORD** that dwells in you. So, every living human being is the *celebrant* of this program. Since you are a *celebrant*, you are not *celebrating* the *celebrant* King Solomon David ETE. You are not *celebrating* any other *celebrant*. You are *celebrating* yourself as the *celebrant*. And that is the reason **The WORD** short-listed you as you recognized **HIM.**

CONCLUSION A:

THE **WORD** FROM SPIRIT TO SOUL AND TO PHYSICAL TRUTH MANIFESTING

You see that? **The WORD** from spirit to soul and to physical truth. As **I** said before, **The WORD** is **THE SPIRIT,** unheard-able, unseen-able and untouchable. Now when you hear the **WORD**, realize that through **The WORD**, **I** become heard-able.

I, THE FATHER GOD made **MY-SELF** heard-able through **The WORD** so, from heard-able to the soul. What is the soul? The soul object is when **The**

WORD says, go and do this. That forms the soul. That is, the imagination of that thing you must do. You can then take that which is in your imagination and creates it physically.

An object soul is in your heart that is, your imagination. From the imagination you have it in physical truth. Then you can lay hand on that thing. You can touch it and you can see it. That is what it is. **I** do not need to dwell too much on this because **I** have revealed so many things about this.

That is the meaning of - **The WORD** from spirit to soul and from soul to physical truth. Everything is like that.

CONCLUSION B:

THE **WORD** OF THINKING

When **I THE FATHER GOD ALMIGHTY** from the Supreme Spirit thought manifest **WORD** it is **The WORD** thinking, speaking, hearing,

writing, processing the WORD, typing, pointing, instructing, signing, singing, looking, fingering WORDS …the endless use of **The WORD**. That is *Conclusion B*. So, show **ME** how you can escape this SUPREME CELEBRATION OF WORD SEASON PROGRAMME.

The WORD is thinking, speaking, hearing, writing, processing, typing, pointing, instructing, signing, singing, looking, fingering WORDS …the endless use of **The WORD**. This is where everybody is captured.

Thinking -You use your heart to think about **The WORD** and that is where **THE FATHER** resides in your system. When **I** say **I, THE FATHER GOD** lives in you, a lot of you argue, because you do not understand. **I** live in you as **The Spirit THOUGHT.** That is **ME, THE FATHER GOD.** So, **I AM** staying there thinking.

Okay! From the thinking **I** speak. When **I** think or do not think but when the hyphen opens the mouth then **I** come out.

Speaking - The **WORD** is speaking from your mouth. Your mouth where the **WORDS** come out from is your body. From you that is, your body **I** was thinking in you. **I** was thinking – in you, now **I AM** *speaking*.

Hearing - Now **I AM** hearing. In you **I AM** hearing. So, if **I AM** hearing in you, don't you know that **I AM** living in you and hearing everything in you? THEREFORE, YOU WILL NOT ESCAPE **ME – O!**

Okay! When **I AM** hearing, what do **I** do next?

Writing - **I AM** writing in you. Is it not **MYSELF** in you using the hand to write? Okay! When **I AM** writing now, what follows?

Processing - **I AM** processing – processing **The WORD**. Whatever you are writing, whatsoever you are doing –

through the instruction of writing or through the instruction that says, by practical demonstration or in any other form is processing. **I AM** processing. Everything is by processing. Petroleum – processing petroleum - before the refinery produced anything processing takes place. Even money is processed. Every situation is processed via **The WORD** via instruction, via writing, via information. Processing is the major action of **The WORD**. All chemicals, all factories, businesses, education and all – everything is by processing the **WORD** – **WORD PROCESSOR.** Everything is processing life. Process - the generality of everything on earth is processing. Processing is **The WORD**.

Typing - Okay! Typing the **WORD** on a keyboard to have the input, when you type, you input the **WORDS**. You type! You put everything there – *inputting* – typing – keyboard. What is that? Who is it that is typing? It is **ME,** in you doing that. If **I** off **MY** air and run away from you and you drop dead, will you still be typing?

Therefore, the **WORD** is all in actions. *Pointing* – if **I** use **MY** finger to point at you or if **I** make the arrow to point at something that is the director and it is **The WORD**.

Pointing to your heart.
Point to your ear.
Point to your nose.
Point to right.
Point to left.
Point to front.
Point to back.
Point up.
Point down.
Point a circular manner.
All the pointing is what? It is of course **The WORD**. So, what is doing the pointing? It is **The WORD**. Who points? It is **ME THE FATHER GOD** in you pointing by **The WORD**.

Okay! After pointing what happens, silently? There must be instructions. Then the next thing is instructing through the pointing.
Point the finger to the wall.
Point the finger to the end of the road.
Point the finger to the right.
Point the finger to the left. Those are instructions. Pointing – stop there!
Pointing – go! Fly! Move! Stop! Come!
All are pointing and directed by instruction.

Signing – What do you do? **I** in you do the signing by appending signature. **I** sign signature whether in spirit or soul. Signing – signing signature - what do **I** use – what is the energy for signing signature?

Signing is **The WORD**. Signing – signature – signatory that is **MY POWER** of **the WORD** so, signing is **The WORD** – the energy of **The WORD**. When **I** sign by stamping and approval appending signature could follow. With that you can instruct to build; you can direct; you can advice; you can write out instructions, directives, and orders and so on, but there must be the signing of signature for authentication and approval. **I** in you is signing that is, appending signature as approval to any required thing.

Will **I** in you therefore, say that **I** in you would not sign this program? Let **ME** see why **I** in you signs all sorts of things – all sorts of rubbish in this world, but when it comes to signing for **ME, I** would refuse to sign. Then that will be the trouble you will have between you and **MYSELF** in you.

Looking – What is looking? Who is the one looking? It is you and **I. ME** and you open your eyes and look, look and look. The hand has finished signing. Now the eye is looking. The ears will be hearing. All parts of your body are manipulated by **The WORD**, ruled by **The WORD**, managed by **The WORD** and controlled by **The WORD**. You hear

The WORD through your ear – hearing. When you hear **The WORD** with your ear, you are looking at **The WORD**. What are you looking at? You look - whether positive or negative you look. That is the light of the world. If you can't look you are in trouble.

When you look, what happens? The thought starts thinking – imagination – describing what you are looking at and what it is. You look at the road – your left and your right, looking forward, looking backward. Everything is by looking – observing. That is **The WORD** directing you to know what you are looking for.

Walking - **The WORD** makes you walk with your legs. You are walking around. It is **The WORD** that manipulates your leg to be walking around. While looking you are walking too.

Seeing - The **WORD** makes you see things with your eyes. That is **THE FATHER GOD** living in you, seeing. All parts of your body system in one way or another serve **The WORD** and administer to **The WORD**. The hands are touching, fingering, typing, pointing and doing all sorts of other things, through **The WORD**.
Your eyes are looking and observing through **The WORD**.
Your ears are hearing through **The WORD**.
Your mouth is talking through **The WORD**.
Speaking, talking, spoken – whatsoever you mean is through **The WORD**.
Walking with your legs to anywhere and even running. All are **The WORD** commanding you and the servant of **The WORD** takes action.

Then fingering, manipulating things, cut and paste – whatsoever you are doing, whether with your brain or hands – designing, sculpturing, moulding, working with woods, engineering – all of them are via **The WORD** directing your body to do that.

So, human being is Servant of God – Servant of **THE ALMIGHTY FATHER GOD** – Servant of **The WORD**. You must appreciate this wisdom – this innovation, **THE UNIVERSAL SUPREME WORD SEASON CELEBRATION.** It is a must!

The WORD is endless and the use of **The WORD** is endless. YOU MUST SHOW APPRECIATION.

CONCLUSION C:

THE WORD SUPREME DIMENSIONS

The **WORD** Supreme dimensions cover the **'*OMNISMS*'**.

Omnisms means omnipotent, omnipresent and omniscience. *Omnisms* cover all aspects of life. That is **THE SUPREME WORD OF THE UNIVERSE** in total dimension that comprise the *omnisms.* Therefore, no human being is exempt. It does not matter that you are foetus in the womb. When you are born, the first sign is life. Even what generates the blood to make the child alive in the womb is **The WORD** that lives in the mother. If the mother dies the child in the womb dies few hours afterwards, because **The WORD** that maintains the child was off.

If somebody is so sick, but **The WORD** is still in the person, it is a sign that the sick person might recover. **The WORD** is **THE FATHER GOD** is **THE SPIRIT** in everybody. Therefore, **I** will talk an endless progressing, promotional talk about The Spoken **WORD**. Indeed very big promotion about **The WORD**. I will stop so far today.

The WORD is all and all and covers everywhere. **The WORD ITSELF** is called the Wide Angle of **THE FATHER GOD** – the Wisdom - **The WORD**. Don't you see Solomon ETE – the wise man? It means **The WORD** lives in him and that is the wisdom. I said that I would not give anybody the blessing I give to Solomon ETE. That means **The WORD** I gave to King Solomon David Jesse ETE '*OFFICE*' – KING SOLOMON SPIRITUAL LIBRARY, COMPREHENSIVE AND ABILITY MEMORY OF THE FATHER GOD IN HIM.

Wisdom means the Wide Angle of God. It is so wide that you cannot see the beginning and end of it. It is so deep that it

defies comprehension. Wisdom is the Wide Angle of **THE FATHER GOD.** Knowledge – cleverness is the nearer angle, which is the female part of wisdom. Today in this **FATHER'S TALK (GOD PRESENT) I** have revealed **MYSELF** and this forms happiness for all positive human beings on earth.
Let **MY** peace and blessing abide with the entire world now and forever more. Amen.
THANK YOU FATHER.

In the Name of Our Lord Jesus Christ
In the Blood of Our Lord Jesus Christ
Now and forever more

THANK YOU FATHER

Chapter Two

MY EVERY REASON

"MY REASONS TO CELEBRATE THE UNIVERSAL SUPREME WORD SEASONS"
By King Solomon David Jesse ETE
ETE ROYAL UNIVERSAL FAMILY

FATHER'S TALK
(GOD PRESENT)

Enoch, Twenty-five Simon Canaanite, FATHER, Two Thousand and Eight (BE/OB/BOOH) Monday, Twenty-five Februray Year Two Thousand and Eight (25/02/2008)

**In the Name of Our Lord Jesus Christ
In the Blood of Our Lord Jesus Christ
Now and forever more**

EVERY REASON

"MY REASONS TO CELEBRATE THE UNIVERSAL SUPREME WORD SEASONS"

EVERY REASON is the title of this Everlasting Testimony Revelation Lecture. This lecture titled **EVERY REASON** is about joining the Universal Supreme Season celebration to appreciate **THE WORD.**

MY REASONS

I have an endless reason to join and celebrate the Universal Supreme Word Season.

First of all, I have to thank **THE FATHER GOD THE CREATOR OF THE UNIVERSE** for making me a living soul and dwell inside me as the Supreme Word of the Universe. I would never know that I owe a lot to my God in all ages until **THE SUPREME CREATOR OF THE UNIVERSE, THE WORD** revealed **HIMSELF** to me that I should celebrate the season – The Supreme Season of appreciation to **THE WORD.** That is my first point of giving **HIM** thanks for the wonderful motivation and the wonderful revelation of all revelations and the wonderful inspiration of all inspirations.

I have never heard yet in the whole universe that anybody has set aside one second, one minute, an hour, a day, a week, a month or a year much more, ever to show appreciation and celebrate **THE**

WORD. Though I have known from the bible that The Word in beginning is with God and The Word is God and that Word is everything and through the Word everything that is made is made. And that without the word nothing would be made, nothing would exist. That is all.

I also heard that The Word became flesh and lived among men and that is what every one else understands. That is, until now that **THE SUPREME FATHER GOD ALMIGHTY,** THE SUPREME SPIRIT, which is **THE WORD** manifested **HIMSELF** and revealed **HIMSELF** in this magnitude.

Then I, HRM King Solomon personally with my family of ETE ROYAL UNIVERSAL FAMILY started to celebrate THE SUPREME WORD OF THE UNIVERSE. Now, **THE FATHER GOD ALMIGHTY** has instructed me officially to extend this gratitude of mind to the entire universe to join the celebration and appreciation of **THE**

WORD. So, all the goodwill human beings, reasonable humans and I mean reasonable human beings should join me for this wonderful universal great movement of all times.

I have every reason to thank **THE FATHER GOD** for this wonderful, magnificent motivation mind of God in me. This is not a human mind. This is not the human way of doing things. It is the Holy Spirit of Truth that manifested **HIMSELF** in this last generation.

As a matter of fact, this is a wonderful generation – the generation of the Glory of God – **The Total Glory Of God.** Since **THE FATHER GOD HIMSELF** has revealed **HIMSELF** in this wonderful way, every human being should be very happy and be so overwhelmed with joy for the wonderful recognition of their CREATOR – **THE SPOKEN WORD** and the only **Administrator** and **Commander In Chief of Heaven and Earth.** Matter of fact, **THE WORD** is ALL and ALL.

Think about it like I am thinking if you are reasonable human being, who has sense, who has impetus of life inside you. If you breathe then you will think. And if you think then you will speak and if you speak then, you will hear and see and if you hear and see, then you will do it well.

You have activities – every activity is relative to **The Word**. Reason with me. Read this '*MY EVERY REASON*' and it could also be your reason for you to join me for this wonderful Universal Movement of Supreme Celebration on earth now established.

This is my thanking **THE FATHER GOD.** It is endless in my heart according to my universal unlimited memory. I do not have word enough to thank and show appreciation. Nonetheless, since **The Word** is everything to use to thank **HIM, THE WORD** is **THE WORD HIMSELF** that will thank **HIM – THE FATHER GOD.**

It is **THE WORD HIMSELF** that will appreciate **THE FATHER GOD** because even if you thank **HIM** and appreciate and join the week and recognize **HIM** you are not the one that is doing it. Directly and indirectly it is **THE WORD** that is doing it because without **THE WORD** living in you kicking, sparkling and tingling, you will not be able to be alive to thank the life. So life must be in you to thank life and that is **THE WORD.**

If you do not see light you cannot see life. You have to have the light to see the life, and also, if you do not have life you cannot witness Light, you have to be alive to witness the Supreme Light of THE UNIVERSAL SUPREME WORD SEASON CELEBRATION FOR THE FIRST TIME HERE ON EARTH. It is wonderful! Is it not so? This is where we see the Wisdom – Super Wisdom of God manifesting physically on earth. **HE** is everything. This is not a matter of claiming to worship God. God is only a word. This is a matter of recognizing **THE WORD,** which is ALL and ALL, THE

TOTALITY OF ALL TOTALITIES. In spirit, in soul and in the physical truth, is **THE WORD**.

So, even if you are Satan, devil, demon, idiot or stupid – all types of negativism - all are **THE WORD.** You must therefore appreciate **THE WORD** or you rather not exist.

Therefore, **THE WORD** Season Celebration is INCLUDED. The title is THE INCLUDED. I am thanking **THE INCLUDED** because it is also round in form, circle in form and O in form. So, wherever you find yourself you are included in this circle, in the O form, in spirit, in soul and the physical. You are inside **THE WORD** and **THE WORD** is inside you. You are therefore included. The circle of **THE WORD** is round and you are inside the word. There is no spirit, soul or human that can escape **THE WORD.** If you die you die in **THE WORD** when you are born you are born in **THE WORD.** If you live, you live in

THE WORD. In the three capacities **THE WORD IS THE SUPREME** – THE UNIVERSAL PHENOMENON.

I thank **THE WORD** so much that even if no human being on earth joined me – maybe by arrogance, pomposity or ignorance or because of stupidity or just unknowingly they refused to join me in this Supreme Universal Celebration Program to honour **THE SUPREME WORD,** I will do it by myself with all those who understand. These are the reasonable human beings.

There is nobody who is not a slave to the **Spoken Word.** No matter how big you are, even if you have seven heads, you are a servant to **THE WORD.** Nobody is exempt even **THE FATHER GOD HIMSELF,** when **HE** materializes in human form **HE** uses **THE WORD.** The Soul of God is **THE WORD.** Everybody's soul is **THE WORD.**

By celebrating **THE SUPREME WORD** you have taken evolution to the higher soul of your life, which is **THE WORD**. You are now triumphant against principalities, if your soul becomes **THE WORD** that is, the Higher Soul. **THE WORD** and you now become one. Anything you say and wish is what will materialize for you. Then you are no more under any principalities or anything in this world since **THE WORD** who is everything is inside you directly and you are in **HIM.** I call **THE WORD** him. I can call **THE WORD** her. I can call **THE WORD** she. I can call **THE WORD** he. Everything is **THE WORD**.

So long as you mention things and think about the word, hear the word or doing the word that is **THE WORD HIMSELF.** Nobody on this earth can explain or expatiating **THE WORD** and appreciate enough, but **THE WORD** is the ONE doing everything for **HIM-SELF.**
If you refuse to join me and join yourself to celebrate it that means **THE WORD** has not given you the privilege.

I thank **THE FATHER GOD** so much because this celebration is the first of its kind. It is a phenomenon that will change the world for good. It is the only celebration that will unite all the creations and bring the whole world together. As a matter of fact, the act of celebrating **THE WORD SEASON** means that you actually recognize who **THE FATHER GOD** is and the reason God said **I** created man in **MY** image and likeness. **GOD is THE WORD. THE WORD is GOOD.** It is only the good things on this earth that is **THE WORD.**

Though we human being uses The Word wrongly, but that does not mean The Word is not good. **THE WORD HIMSELF** is extremely good. **THE WORD** is the most excellent of goodness, because what you wish is what **THE WORD** wishes you. **THE WORD** has never wished anybody any evil. It is only when you think evil and speak evil then you wish yourself that but if you change that to good then **THE**

WORD also wishes you good. What is ALL and ALL is INCLUDED.

As I am talking about **THE WORD,** I am so overwhelmed and taken over completely by **THE WORD HIMSELF. THE WORD** talks of **THE WORD. THE WORD** speaks of **THE WORD** – talking, talking, and talking.
I have **EVERY REASON** to testify about **THE WORD.** I have **EVERY REASON** to celebrate **THE WORD** and I have **EVERY REASON** to appreciate **THE WORD.**
I am thinking – is **THE WORD.**
I am speaking – is **THE WORD.**
I am hearing – is **THE WORD.**
I am writing – is **THE WORD.**
I am walking - is **THE WORD.**
I am looking - is **THE WORD.**
I am talking – is **THE WORD.**
I am pointing - is **THE WORD.**
I am moving – is **THE WORD.**
I am seeing – is **THE WORD.**
I am going – is **THE WORD.**
I am coming –is **THE WORD.**

I am standing –is **THE WORD.**
I am sitting –is **THE WORD.**
I am meeting –is **THE WORD.**
I am making –is **THE WORD.**
I am torching –is **THE WORD.**
I am singing –is **THE WORD.**
I am smiling –is **THE WORD**
I am dancing –is **THE WORD**
I am praying –is **THE WORD.**
I am taking –is **THE WORD**
I am giving –is **THE WORD**
I am living –is **THE WORD**
Using my Fingers and Fingering things around – is **THE WORD.** Thinking faculty, reasoning faculty – all are **THE WORD.** My heart is where **THE WORD** resides and takes over all parts of my body.

THE WORD is all things to me and everything to me. **THE WORD** means Brotherhood. **THE WORD** means ALL and ALL. The Father of **THE WORD** is **THE SPIRIT** that motivates the word and motivates the thoughts. So **THE**

FATHER GOD is **THE SPIRIT** that manifests **THE WORD.**

I understand through understanding and the Intelligent Super Wisdom from my Supreme Memory – the Comprehensive and Ability Memory of God in me that **HE IS THE SPIRIT** is unheard-able, unseen-able and untouchable. Now, that **SPIRIT** before it becomes heard-able it is via **The Word**. That was why **HE** projected **HIMSELF** as the sound and formed Gen of all things, The Spoken and that is the amplifier of **SOUND** that manifested **THE WORD**. And because **THE WORD** is now manifested, the **SPIRIT** becomes heard-able. Through **THE SPIRIT** being heard, **HE** becomes seen-able and seen-able becomes touchable which now become man and every other creation, including, organisms and living creatures.

THE WORD is the Supreme Creator that created all living creatures and all living organisms, including non-living organisms and motivates them. Then man now creates the things that are not spirit, but physical and mundane creations. We must bring all mundane creations together to appreciate **THE WORD.**

Therefore, the appreciation of **THE SUPREME WORD** has no beginning and it has no end. It is for eternity. We must all therefore show appreciation to **THE FATHER GOD** for everything that **HE** has done and is doing. **THE SUPREME WORD OF THE UNIVERSE** formulated every creation seen and unseen, touchable and not touchable, heard-able and unheard-able.

All things that God created are not perishable, because they are living organisms and living creatures. But everything that mankind creates are perishable – from aeroplane to motorcars and other moving engines, computer ideas and other technology like the word equipments for instance, - the Software and the Hardware, chairs, tables and all the rest of them. Yes, everything man creates as image and likeness of God perishes, except **Microsoft Word** by Bill Gate.

What is the meaning of image and likeness of God in man? Man physical body is image (PHOTO OR PICTURE), and the likeness of GOD in man is **THE WORD (SPIRIT).** Since **THE FATHER GOD HIMSELF** creates, man also creates. Man is God in human form. You will agree with me from now till eternity that the stupidity and ignorance of man have finished since **THE FATHER GOD** has come to take **HIS** glory.

Every human being should learn a lesson from that part of elementary stage of life that refused to acknowledge this idea of appreciation of **THE WORD.** Even in Heaven I understand through the understanding of the Supreme Wisdom of God in me that the reason **THE FATHER GOD** sent Lucifer away from heaven to become a roam about spirit up till today is because she refused to appreciate and acknowledge **THE WORD.** I understand also through my memory records that **THE SUPREME SPIRIT** when **HE** was unheard-able called **HIMSELF** in all totality, because everything you see that manifested already existed in the thought and that is **THE SUPREME SPIRIT OF THE FATHER GOD.**

I understand that when that **Supreme Thought** called **HIMSELF** and had meeting with all **SELVES** that **THE WORD** should be the overseer and represent all things that are not yet seen-able, not touchable and unheard-able. One of the **SELVES** who was Lucifer and was the second in command disagreed with that idea.

She disagreed in the sense that **THE WORD** would be glorified more than any other. Being that she was the elementary part of **THE FATHER GOD** she did not understand that, if you promote your child and honour your child; indirectly you honour yourself, because that is your continuity.

It is only **THE FATHER GOD** that knows the secret of **HIS** Kingdom. Since God is Wisdom **HIMSELF, HE** knew that by promoting your child you are also promoting yourself, because every child answers his or her father's surname and your father answered his father's surname and that goes on endlessly being the continuity.

So, if you condemn your child you automatically condemn your future unless that child condemns you and if that child condemned his father he also condemned his endless future, but the positive father or positive son will take spiritual evolution into his new arrange and continuation of live. Then that mean you have to find a different way to register your future continuation. Because of this oxymoron spirit Lucifer failed the final, final failure because **THE FATHER GOD** with other selves agreed that they wanted their selves – their own portion of **FATHER GOD** in them to be recognized on earth, in the physical reality. For that reason they signed on with **THE FATHER GOD** and honour **THE WORD,** celebrate **THE WORD** and appreciate **THE WORD.**

When Abel therefore manifested, he took up that entity while Cain took up the other entity. So, Abel recognized **THE WORD,** celebrated **THE WORD** and appreciated **THE WORD.** With that he became the righteous Abel till tomorrow forever and ever. Cain refused to appreciate **THE WORD** because he took oxymoron's spirit.

When Cain refused to honour **THE WORD** nobody heard about him. He lost it all and when you lose by **THE WORD** you are lost for eternity. That point is what we call Satan, devil, demon and elementary spirit. It is a mistake that you know if you make, you can never forgive yourself for eternity.

So my dear brethren do not make this same mistake by using pomposity, your big man status or your position. Whosoever you think you are, you are not greater than **THE ONE** who created you. So if you refuse to join me to do this celebration of all times – The Supreme Celebration season throughout your life time, then you will never forgive your soul for eternity, just like Lucifer. That is the only help I can render in this my word of I have **EVERY REASON.**

I thank **THE FATHER GOD** for the ability to join the Universal Supreme Word Celebration and appreciate **THE WORD** here on earth. I have made a will – a vow to my soul - from my spirit to my soul, and from my soul to my physical reality in truth my physical present, that at any time, any second, any minute, any hour, any day, any month, any year and anytime for everlasting, this is going to be my job, to celebrate, recognize and appreciate **THE SUPREME WORD OF THE UNIVERSE** for eternity as my all and all. When I do this directly and indirectly I have recognized **THE FATHER GOD THE CREATOR OF THE UNIVERSE** which is **THE SUPREME SPIRIT** –unheard-able, unseen-able and untouchable that became heard-able seen-able and touchable through **THE WORD.**

So my dear brothers and sisters, **THE WORD** is everything for me and I have nothing enough to appreciate **THE WORD,** but I have everything to celebrate and appreciate **THE WORD.** Why? Because whatsoever I am it is **THE WORD** that is that. Whatsoever I am, **THE WORD** is **I AM THAT I AM.** For that reason I have no cause to be alarmed. Nevertheless, I can only do my best in any circumstance to give my full thanksgiving and show appreciation to **THE WORD** and celebrate **THE WORD** in the new season of Universal Supreme Word Celebration on earth. Thank **YOU FATHER.**

CELEBRANTS OF THE WORD

I wish all the celebrants good-luck. I am the celebrant you are the celebrant. I have to explain a point here. I know a lot of people will ask certain questions. Like who is supposed to be the head of the celebrants of **THE WORD** since nobody sees **THE WORD.** Who should be the person to coordinate this celebration?

THE WORD HIMSELF has chosen somebody – a human person to coordinate the celebration. As you all know everything has a head. The inspirational person of this program is the one that **THE WORD** has chosen with all admiration, approval and seal, stamped and signed by **THE FATHER GOD** to coordinate all things that are connected to **THE SUPREME WORD** season celebration and appreciation. More so, **THE FATHER GOD HIMSELF** has given the instructions on how every process should be handled.

First of all, you must understand that every human being is a celebrant since **THE WORD** lives in you. And it is only human beings that God permitted to be the celebrants of this celebration. Other living creatures that cannot say meaningful words are just to join in the celebration, but not as the celebrants. Every other living creatures and living organisms are other things used to support the celebration.

Therefore, when you eat the living organisms and they give you energy of life – supporting energy of life and maintain **THE WORD** in you, then that is another way to support you to celebrate **THE WORD.** But the living creatures, which is man in four capacities and four stages – human-fish, human-bird, human-animal and the real humans – the Human-Gods, all must join hands together for the celebration. Therefore, you are all celebrants.

Since you are celebrant you should not use again what you used as an appreciation, but you can benefit through the program. The proceeds from the program should be used to cater for the entire human kind. This celebration season program will be used to raise fund for all incurable diseases because it is only **THE FATHER GOD** that takes care of **HIS** children and cares about **HIS** children. **THE WORD** is **THE FATHER. THE WORD** is the mother.

THE WORD is the brother. **THE WORD** is the sister. **THE WORD** is your family relation.

Do not think you love anybody too much because you are the president or because you are King or you are Lord. You cannot do anything. It is only **THE WORD** that does everything. So if you use this umbrella to establish that firmly on earth, when you are not here physically, **THE WORD** will continue with the celebration and you will come back to join it. If you use your name or position to do it, when you are no more in that position that is the end of your programme.

People have been using goodwill to launch this and to launch that and raise all sorts of funds – for cancer, disasters and other diseases – HIV and so on. When the money is collected some people use the money for something else or misappropriate the fund in so many ways. Some people when they are in such positions when they die the program ends.

Some others raise funds and use the proceeds for political purposes. Those are elementary aspect of things.

You should bring all of them under this universal umbrella for every soul and the universal bank account is sufficient for every soul. It is called **IN and OUT** account for all mankind. When you are capable you appreciate **THE WORD.** When you become incapable, then **THE WORD** takes care of you. Every human being must register and show appreciation. It is a universal spiritual bank that will never finish. You deposit there for yourself, so that you can have it there also for yourself.

Therefore, everybody is a celebrant. As you can see from the directives of usage of the proceeds via **THE FATHER GOD'S** instructions that His Royal Majesty King Solomon Etteh is the one to do it and direct the programme, because people would say oh, another Nigerian man.

I am not a Nigerian of that sort. I am a Universal Man – Ete Royal Universal Family. I came from a Universal Phenomenon - **THE WORD, THE FATHER GOD ALMIGHTY** and I stand under that. However, it happened that the centre that I fall in germination is in Nigeria. Where there is carcass there are vultures. There is a reason for that. I saw in spirit why so many great men and women - great souls manifest in Nigeria. You never know where your next call of manifestation will be. If you are positive you could be among the great men and women in Nigeria. For wherever there is carcass there are vultures.

Therefore where your gold and silver is your heart is there. There must be something in Nigeria which is not negative that attracts all great hearts – all great buildings of the spiritual world to manifest in Nigeria. Look at it well the second time. Check the people. It is not every Nigerian that dupes. It is not every Nigerian preacher that is fake, and not all the people that you see doing one thing or the other that are bad. It is just that bad people find themselves there because what attracts them is Light. Where there is good bad always go there. Nonetheless, good always triumphs against bad, because the power of light destroys darkness automatically.

So Nigeria, which the whole world terms to be the worst criminal centre, very soon, will be known as the most save place on earth. This is where **THE FATHER GOD** manifested **HIMSELF** as **THE SUPREME WORD.** Whether you like it or not, The Truth remains The Truth – unchangeable in nature.

When you say one plus one is equal to two, it is everlasting truth. There is no way you can manipulate it your way to say that one plus one is three or four or one hundred or even one. So, one added to another one must become two. Therefore, try and do your homework well. If you are spirit search the memory of spiritual things. If you are anything of reckoning checks things out. When you then see and discover anything come and speak the truth. If you betray The Truth as you know about The Truth, The truth will query you and then you will be in trouble. You will be put in the wastebasket and you are one of the oxymoron, because Lucifer refused to accept The Truth. The untruth will not set you free but whoever accepts The Truth, The Truth will set that person free.

THE SPIRIT of THE WORD is the Positive Spirit called **THAT SPIRIT,** which is liberty itself and where that spirit is there is liberty. So **THE SPIRIT** is liberty. Great men that manifested in Nigeria will soon recognize themselves. However, many Nigerians join the bad part of the whole matter, because they are afraid of what Satan did to Christ.

When Christ manifested on earth if HE did not know HIMSELF Satan - the same Lucifer would have betrayed Christ. He knew that HE was **THE WORD** that manifested and the Creator of everything on earth both spirit and physical. He took

Christ to the mountain to tempt Him. It was **THE FATHER GOD** that gave that negative spirit the ability. He was also the word, just as the word in you tests you, one is positive and the other is negative. When the negative word conquers your heart, you do wrong thing. When the positive Word conquers your heart then you do good thing.

They are all in your heart. It was through the heart that Lucifer tempted Christ. That voice was His heart. When Lucifer took Christ to the mountain and the desert – where there was no water and no food and no shelter, Christ was miserable physically, but **THE FATHER GOD** was in Him.

When He became too hungry, the negative self said to him, you have power to command this stone to turn to bread. Why do you suffer this hunger? Are you not the Creator? Are you not the Word? Just command this stone to turn to bread for you to eat. If Christ had commanded that stone to turn to bread, it would be artificial bread. It would not be the real bread. It would not be the leaven bread.

The stone that the command would turn to bread would be elementary bread. If Christ ate the bread, it would be inside our Lord Jesus Christ as negative and that would have been witchcraft spirit. All magic is witchcraft. Any fantasy is witchcraft. Something that does not exist but you produce it that is fantasy, that is witchcraft. It is nothingness, counterfeit, elementary.

So the higher self of Jesus Christ, which is **THE WORD** in **HIM** which is **THE FATHER GOD THE SPIRIT HIMSELF**, because **HE** knew who that was and revealed her and said – man lives not only by bread but by **THE WORD** inside himself.

Enye! Odudu! Abasi mi! Zim, zim, zim! Assassu!

The higher self grew and overwhelmed and became triumphant over the other one and that one died. Another one came and said – why do you suffer here and look

you are on top of the mountain, throw down yourself. You will not die because we are all serving you, angels and all including me, Lucifer we will hold you well. But they were all ready to be wicked to Christ. Jesus Christ answered and said – No you cannot tempt your God.
Then the third one came and said to Christ, I know you are king but I own everything in this world, this mundane world. All the money and everything else I own them because **THE FATHER GOD** sent me down here to control them. So they are all in my hand, as you have come to take over this world just bow down for me even for one second. Just recognize me for one second then you own the whole thing.

The negative self speaks the word, but does not mean it. That is the kind of word that some politicians speak. That is the word that evil people speak - when you speak words that you do not mean to take seriously. As your thoughts are different from your speech, you are representing Satan.

Satan wanted Christ – the higher self to bow down for him and if Christ did, he would say now you have bowed down to me you have no powers again. You have surrendered to me. Just like how men would deceive some women to sleep with them. They would promise them heaven and earth and would say 'I will marry you'.

If you know that the woman is so much eager to get married to you – maybe because you are handsome or rich and she wanted to claim you, then you deceive that woman by promising to marry her. Then you give her an engagement ring. What is the meaning of engagement ring?

What obtains today is people marry in the morning and divorce in the evening because by then they've gotten what they wanted. Both men and women engage in this sordid game of motive and intention with pretentiousness. They think different, speak different and do different thing all together. All three capacities are different.

On the contrary, the truth spirit in you – **THE WORD, THE POSITIVE WORD** will think and the same thinking will materialize the same word and the same word will materialize the same activity that is, the same event of action.

As the **SUPREME WORD** conquered that negative mind, today this is the result, which is the celebration, the appreciation and the recognition of the **SUPREME WORD – CHRIST** for eternity.

So, do not go back to think who will eat the money – who will manage the money? When you use **THE WORD** to create your office and to do all sorts of things who asks you questions? That is the reason you are asked now, to appreciate **THE WORD**. The thing you use in you, the energy in you to materialize and gain from it, you should show appreciation.

THE WORD has not told you to go and steal for **HIM**. **THE WORD** has not sent you to go and kill people for **HIM**. **THE WORD** says anything in your possession, whatsoever that is your positive endeavour, the energy you derive and gain from your personal life and not the life of another person, and you must appreciate **THE WORD** with it.

When you do that you do the correct thing. When you refuse to do that then, your life - the life in you - **THE WORD** in you - the life will query your life. And you will have everlasting guilty conscience, which you will never forgive your life when your eyes opened, now and forever more. Amen.

Then the last point is that I will say some few words regarding this idea about what God revealed.

I am thinking
I am speaking
I am hearing
I am working
I am writing
I am touching and fingering things with my fingers
I am looking with my eyes

I am even eating – opening my mouth and putting food.

I am walking on the road and touching things and pointing at things. Thinking anything, doing anything, speaking anything – the generality of everything are directed and motivated by the life in me, which is **THE WORD.** That thing that made me alive – the beam of life, is **THE WORD.** Without it instructions would not be given. I would not hear, I would not talk, I would not fingering things with my fingers, I would not writing **THE WORD. THE WORD** manipulates the concept of every situation and everything. Therefore, I have **EVERY REASON** to celebrate and appreciate with The Universal Supreme Word Season celebration through out eternity. Wherever I am – in any planet, in spirit, in soul and physical, whenever I take assumed body in this planet that will be my duty.

I, His Royal Majesty King Solomon David Jesse Etteh, I know through this super memory I discovered who I was in the past, who I am in the present and future. This has nothing to do with elementary spirits. This has nothing to do with any secret society.

All of you out there should ask anybody - ask your old Masters and check in your records whether you can see my name there. Go to the witchcraft world and check whether you will see me there. If you ever see me there, that means **THE FATHER GOD ALMIGHTY HIMSELF** that is there for discovery of souls, and to destroy the evils with **HIS** present of the supreme Light of the Holy Spirit of Truth.

Any day and in any form **THE WORD – THE FATHER GOD** manifest as Light and come to any darkness and evil places that is the end of that place. However, you won't see me there in your record. Check all the secret societies you belong to, ask your masters or any spirit that is directing you there, and ask if I am a member there. Since you are using **THE WORD** to manipulate those situations, **THE WORD** is a member there. And **THE WORD** is inspector general of that place. And **THE WORD** knows everything you are doing. So if you are using **THE WORD** in elementary way – in an evil manner, **THE WORD** is now querying you. And **HE** has banned it outright! So retrace your steps and come back to positivism!

I am a man of positivism. I am Abel and other subsequent transits. Then I was King Solomon of Israel and then King James of the United Kingdom. Now I am King Solomon David Jesse Etteh. **THE WORD** told me who I was before now and I believe it because **THE WORD IS THE ONLY TRUTH.**

It is only that when you betray **THE WORD,** you give accounts. **THE WORD** is Supreme Auditor. **THE WORD** will audit you. Anything you do in your life, **THE WORD** will come and audit you and then the truth manifests. That is why people pay for what they have done.

When you are doing something illegal, you have no problems because nobody audits you. So, you can write to manipulate the papers and eat the church money or organization money, eat government money because you are in charge and nobody audits you. However, **THE WORD** audits every human being. 'By thy **WORD** ye shall be condemned and by thy **WORD** ye shall be justified'. **THE WORD** lives in your conscience. Every human being that is alive has conscience. Even if you can't talk, you are thinking. The last thing man cannot be deprived of is the ability of thinking.

Even when spirit possesses you and you do things questionable and you are not able to account for your actions because you are not of yourself, then **THE WORD** will judge that spirit.

Therefore, everything that I do and these things I have said – this idea, if I am possessed by elementary spirit and the idea ensued thereon, I will be judged through that elementary spirit. **THE WORD** will judge me.

However, if this motivation, this idea and everything I do in my life bring glory – absolute glory to **THE SUPREME WORD OF THE UNIVERSE** because they are positive as the positive spirit that possesses me, then **THE WORD HIMSELF** will give me the blessing in myself. And **THE WORD** will continue to elevate **HIMSELF** in me and make me **HIS** very OWN Divine House. For I believe that King Solomon built house to contain God but God does not live in the house built by man. Even this world cannot contain God. That is the reason **THE WORD** is spirit, soul and physical.

Therefore, there is no need for me to say I have to build a temple for God, which I know God will not live there. As it is God decided to live inside me as **HIS OWN** temple because that was the preparation. I am convinced beyond any doubt that I am the Temple of **THE WORD.** The Living God dwells in me. So every thought, every word I speak and every

hearing is positive and that manifests my activities to be positive on this earth.
Let my thanks and my heart of appreciation of **THE WORD** expressed in this - I have **EVERY REASON** be accepted by the **SUPREME WORD OF THE UNIVERSE, THE FATHER GOD THE CREATOR OF THE UNIVERSE,** now and forever more. Amen.

**In the Name of Our Lord Jesus Christ,
In the Blood of Our Lord Jesus Christ
Now and forever more**

THANK YOU FATHER.

Songs:

A. *I have every reason
    I have every reason
    I have every reason to appreciate the word*

   *I have every reason
   I have every reason*

I have every reason to appreciate the word

  (Repeat x-times)

B.

*Celebrate -o, celebration
The universal celebration of The Word*

*Celebration, celebration of The Word
The Word season celebration of The Word*

*Celebration, celebration of The Word
The Word season celebration of the Word*

*Celebration, celebration of The Word
The Word Season
The Supreme Season celebration of The Word*

*Celebrate The Word
Appreciate The Word
Celebration, celebration of the word*

*The Word season celebration of the
Word*

*Celebration, celebration
The Supreme Season celebration of
The Word*

*Celebration, celebration
The Supreme Season celebration of
The Word*
   (Repeat x-times)

*Celebrate the Word of God
Celebrate The Maker
The Supreme Season celebration of
The Word*

*The Word is The Maker
The Word is the Creator
Celebration, celebration
The Supreme Season celebration of
The Word*

Celebration, celebration

*The Supreme Season celebration of
The Word*

*Celebration, celebration
The Supreme Season celebration of
The Word*

*The Word is your Maker
The Word is your Father
The supreme season celebration of
the word
Celebration, celebration
The Supreme Season celebration of
The Word*
     (Repeat x-times)

*Celebrate the word
Thank the word of God
The Supreme season Celebration of
The Word*

*Celebration, appreciation day
The Supreme Season celebration of
The Word*

Celebration, appreciate The Word
The Supreme Season celebration of
The Word

Celebration, celebration
The Supreme Season celebration of
The Word
    (Repeat x-times)

C. *Let every soul come together*
Every soul, come together
And appreciate The Father God

Let every soul come together
Come together
And show appreciation to the Supreme word
    (Repeat x-time)

The Word is The Creator
The Creator of mankind
The Word is the Creator of the world
Let every soul come together
Come together

And show appreciation to the Supreme Word

*The Supreme of Word of the Universe
The Supreme Word is the Creator
Show appreciation to the Supreme Word
Let every soul come together
Every soul, come together
And appreciate The Father God*

*The Supreme word of Mankind
The Holy Father
We must show appreciation to the Supreme Word
Let every soul come together
Every soul, come together
And appreciate The Father God*

*The Word is your life
The word is everything to mankind
Let every soul come together
And show appreciation to the Supreme Word*

*The Word of the Word of the Word
Of the universe
The Word is life to every man
The word is everything to every soul*

*Without the word the world will not exist
Without the word mankind will not exist
Without the word life will not exist
Let every soul come together
And show appreciation to the Supreme Word...*

*I have every reason
I have every reason
To show appreciaton to the Supreme Word*

The Supreme Word
Celebration! Celebration! Celebration!

D. *He's the Supreme Word OOO
He's the Supreme Word
The Word of the universe*

Leader Olumba Olumba Obu

*He's the Supreme Word OOO
He's the Supreme Word
The Word of the universe
Leader Olumba Olumba Obu*

Song:
  *I have every reason, every reason
  To thank The Word*

  *I have every reason, every reason
  To appreciate The Word*

  *I have every reason, every reason
  To thank The Father*

  *I have every reason, every reason
  To give thanks The Word*

*I have every reason, every reason
  To give thanks to God
  The Father!*

THANK YOU FATHER

Chapter Four

THE VOICE OF THE CREATOR OF THE UNIVERSE
===================

The Supreme Celebration & Bylove of Word

FATHER'S TALK
(GOD PRESENT)

Enoch, Sixteenth James, FATHER Two Thousand and Eight (AF.OF.OH) (Monday, Sixteenth June, Year Two Thousand and Eight (16.06.2008))

In the Name of Our Lord Jesus Christ, In the Blood of Our Lord Jesus Christ, Now and forever more

THE VOICE OF THE CREATOR OF THE UNIVERSE THE FATHER GOD ALMIGHTY TO ALL HUMAN BEINGS ON EARTH

This is the **VOICE OF THE CREATOR OF THE UNIVERSE THE FATHER GOD ALMIGHTY** to all human beings on earth. ***This is the final information and the last remedy to solve the universal Problems of mankind: natural disasters, sickness, and conflicts, wars between nations, disagreements, reporting of many incidents of death and general destruction on earth.***

A: **I, THE FATHER GOD THE CREATOR OF THE UNIVERSE** deserve recognition and total acknowledgement as **THE SUPREME FATHER** who creates and owns all spirits, souls, angels, humans and everything created seen and unseen

B: All **MY** creations should have the total belief in **ME THE SUPREME FATHER GOD THE CREATOR OF THE UNIVERSE**, and refrain completely from worshipping of idols, elementary spirits of any kind, practicing wickedness of any form, and you have to disassociate yourself completely from any negativism and incantations.

C: Everyone should join His Royal Majesty King Solomon David Jesse ETE, the original incarnate of Abel, the positive son of Adam and Eve to celebrate and appreciate **ME, THE SUPREME FATHER GOD ALMIGHTY**, through the universal programme of the **UNIVERSAL SUPREME WORD SEASON CELEBRATION**, which is a yearly event.
I AM THE UNIVERSAL SUPREME WORD, the **MOTIVATOR** of **LIFE** and **LIGHT** of **LIFE SUPREME ENERG**Y. Therefore, any living soul that rejected this order has himself or herself to blame because of the

universal testing programme that **I AM** going to start, in spirit, soul and physical, to shake the world, to remove all shakeable things away, and then all the positive things shall remain on earth.

It has pleased **ME, THE FATHER GOD THE CREATOR OF THE UNIVERSE** to have long patience, longest of all long patience and up till this time. All human beings, all the kings and Queens, Heads of States, Presidents, Governors, daughters and sons of all human beings give deaf ears to **ME** and **MY WORD OF LOVE**, and all the preaching **I** have been passing through **MY** positive Servants to delivered. They still treat the world as though it belongs to them – with total power of evil, still maintain that there is nothing like **THE FATHER GOD THE OWNER OF THE UNIVERSE**.

The whole world has refused to acknowledge **MY** presence as the **SUPREME WORD, THE SUPREME SPIRIT**, and the Owner of ALL things. They rather worship negativism. They worship mermaids and elementary spirits soul instead of their **CREATOR**. **I** have no other option than to exercise **MY** Ownership on earth in whatsoever form **I** like from now on.

So, what human beings will see on earth from now onwards, starting from a very limited time and nobody should predict time for **ME**, they should not doubt.
Nobody knows **MY** will. **I** will do what **I** want and select the positive and destroy all negatives in spirit, soul and physical present. Therefore, in spirit and in soul, if you give deaf ear to this information then, **I** repeat! You have yourself to blame and your soul and your blood will be upon you.
I do everything to salvage mankind and to save your soul, because **I** know the problem you will face if your

soul falls into darkness hell. It is so severe. Everlasting punishment is so severe, which **I** do not wish any of **MY** creations to face. That is why being that **I AM LOVE, I** always bring remedy to mankind in the time like this on earth. So, this is the last and the final remedy, **THE VOICE OF THE CREATOR** to you all **MY** creations.

What was done in Heaven should be done on earth, which was the pleading of the higher positive spirit soul of Adam, which is our Lord Jesus Christ that, what happened in Heaven should also occur here on earth. So, now this is what will happen here on earth: Every soul, every human being will join to celebrate **_THE_**

UNIVERSAL SUPREME WORD SEASON and recognize **THE FATHER GOD** in all aspects of life and shun all negativism. Without that well...! This is your last chance.

THE UNIVERSAL SUPREME WORD SEASON CELEBRATION covers the following celebration criteria and appreciations –

A: Celebrate and appreciate **THE FATHER GOD THE CREATOR OF THE UNIVERSE**

B: Celebrate and appreciate the first human beings Adam and Eve, our first father and mother, the universal Parents of all human beings (BROTHERHOOD) on earth

C: Celebrate and appreciate the positive life – our lives on earth.

D: Celebrate and appreciate **THE FATHER GOD** The divine breathe of life in you – your personal life.

E: Celebrate and appreciate **THE FATHER GOD** the soul of life in you – your personal soul.

F: Celebrate and appreciate **THE FATHER GOD** for sound health – your human physical presence here on earth.

G: Celebrate and appreciate **THE FATHER GOD** for **HIS** love, peace, mercy, kindness, equality, goodwill, righteousness, joy and happiness, long life and prosperity and the rest of all **HIS** good countless goodness for mankind.

H: Celebrate and appreciate **THE FATHER GOD** for **HIS** positive **DIVINE SELF, THE HOLY SPIRIT OF TRUTH, HE** is the **SPIRIT** of all things **BROTHERHOOD**

I: Celebrate and appreciate **THE FATHER GOD, HIS** Divine positive soul. **HE** is the **WORD**, the Supreme Word of the Universe.

AO: Celebrate and appreciate **THE FATHER GOD**, for **HIS** Positive Divine Power, the Holy Spirit of Truth personified on Earth.

THE CELEBRANT-

EVERY HUMAN BEING IS A CELEBRANT

The above are the reasons that every human being is a celebrant of ***THE UNIVERSAL SUPREME WORD SEASON CELEBRATION***. Therefore, it is a must and compulsory that every living soul, especially human kind to do this programme with all their heart. This is the only way **I, THE FATHER GOD THE UNIVERSAL SUPREME WORD, THE CREATOR OF THE UNIVERSE** will give you credit that you recognize **MY EXISTENT AS THE FATHER GOD ALMIGHTY YOUR CREATOR.**

Nevertheless, this can only be done if you love one another and appreciate another life like life in you. Also you appreciate **ME THE FATHER GOD, THE SUPREME WORD** that lives in every soul by respecting and value another life, all live and all living creatures.

Let my peace and blessing abide with the entire world, now and forever more. Amen.

In the Name of Our Lord Jesus Christ, In the Blood of Our Lord Jesus Christ, Now and forever more

THANK YOU FATHER.

Chapter Five

THE INSPIRATIONAL WRITER
=======================

KING SOLOMON SPIRITUAL LIBRARY
THE GOD
ENCYCLOPAEDIA
WORD OF INFINITY

INSPIRATIONAL WRITERS AND READERS OF THE
FATHER'S TALK
(GOD PRESENT)
KING SOLOMON SPIRITUAL LIBRARY

In the name of our Lord Jesus Christ, In the blood of our Lord Jesus Christ, Now and forever more, Amien

(A) REFERENCING THE FATHER'S TALK (GOD PRESENT) IN KING SOLOMON SPIRITUAL LIBRARY

I know that some people will be inspired when they visit King Solomon Spiritual Library website or bookshop, and have access to any of **THE FATHER'S TALK (GOD PRESENT)** information through books, electronics, audio and otherwise and are inspired to write or produce any information through the knowledge that they have gained, they must not fail to reference **THE FATHER'S TALK (GOD PRESENT)** in **King**

Solomon Spiritual Library as the source of your inspirations.

(B) THE WORD OF TRUTH AND THE HOLY SPIRIT PRINCIPLES

Since **THE FATHER'S TALK (GOD PRESENT)** is the direct information from **I THE FATHER GOD ALMIGHTY HIMSELF**, all positive children of **GOD** can be, and will be inspired with this **WORD** because the **WORD** of **THE FATHER GOD, THE CREATOR OF THE UNIVERSE** is a Spiritual Case Study for all souls to improve to have self awareness and a Higherself Consciousness.

When you are inspired and you want to write, make sure that your ideas, principles and concepts are based on the Holy Spirit of Truth without changing the ordinance of the **FATHER'S TALK (GOD PRESENT)**.

(C) THERE SHALL BE CONSEQUENCES THAT WOULD FOLLOW THOSE WHO USE THE MEANING, THE CONCEPTS AND THE PRINCIPLES OF THE FATHER'S TALK (GOD PRESENT) FOR THE PURPOSES OF MISLEADING

Consequences shall follow those who use the meaning, the concepts and the principles of **THE FATHER'S TALK (GOD**

PRESENT) for the purposes of misleading in any manner.

Any Human-God, human-animal, human-bird or human-fish who has access to **THE FATHER'S TALK** (**GOD PRESENT**) through any means, be it via books, electronics, audio and otherwise should know that those words are not the words of human beings. The words are transcribed, proofread and accepted by **ME THE FATHER GOD** as it comes from the **SUPREME STUDIO OF THE ALMIGHTY FATHER GOD HIMSELF**, via **King Solomon Spiritual Library**.

When the signal of the information alerts HRM King Solomon David Jesse **ETE** from **I THE FATHER** through the **COMPREHENSIVE MEMORY OF GOD** in Him, at anytime in the day or at night and anywhere, whether on the road or any public place, he will take note of the title of the Revelation Lectures. Sometimes if the location is conducive, lectures can take place immediately. If the location is not conducive, **I THE FATHER GOD** fixes the time for the full Lecture Revelation to take place. Most of the time, some of the Lecture Revelations take about a week, a month or six months and so on, to deliver when **I THE FATHER GOD** brings it back from **HIS SUPREME MEMORY** to HRM King Solomon **ETE**.

Take note that the information of **THE FATHER'S TALK** (**GOD PRESENT**) is not preaching, or the giving of sermons or shared discussion. **THE FATHER GOD** calls them "***LECTURE***

***REVELATIONS**"*, which is a Spiritual Case Study for humankind to improve and have the Higherself Consciousness about himself or herself and their **CREATOR**.

For this reason, every human being that comes across any of the information of the **FATHER'S TALK** (**GOD PRESENT**) should treat it with utmost and absolute respect and reverence at all times.

HRM King Solomon David Jesse **ETE** is not responsible for **THE FATHER'S TALK** (**GOD PRESENT**) but **ME, THE FATHER GOD HIMSELF. I, THE ALMIGHTY FATHER** only use Him as a way through, just like a loud speaker from the radio or television receiver.

For this reason, HRM King Solomon David Jesse **ETE** will not be held responsible by anyone who does not understand the contents, the concepts and the principles of **THE FATHER'S TALK (GOD PRESENT)** information in King Solomon Spiritual Library. He will not answer any questions or queries from spirit to soul and the physical truth in connection to the above from the lower mind individuals, persons or groups. However, if you are positive and you have love and are humble, have patience and are peaceful and you want to know and understand more of any part of **THE FATHER'S TALK (GOD PRESENT)**; '**You should use fasting and prayer**' and or if anyone has any questions in good faith, he or she is free to write to HRM King Solomon and **THE FATHER** in him will respond. He will not, and there is no response to any questions, queries and anything negative with the craftiness of the evil minds of humankind.

That is why you should first read seven **FATHER'S TALK (GOD PRESENT)** Lecture Revelations before commenting and

THE FATHER GOD with **HIS SUPREME HOLY SPIRIT OF TRUTH** will bless all those who read and accept this information with good faith through the name and blood of our Lord Jesus Christ, *Amien*.

In the name of our Lord Jesus Christ In the blood of our Lord Jesus Christ Now and forever more, Amen

ESTABLISH MY SPIRITUAL LIBRARY

I THE FATHER GOD ALMIGHTY THE SUPREME WORD OF THE UNIVERSE AM THE SPIRITUAL FOOD TO FEED YOUR SOUL. Therefore, **I** want every family in this world, every home in this world, every office, government offices, monarchies, countries, states, regions, counties, communities, local authority compounds, family homes and everyone and everywhere to collect published copies of **THE EVERLASTING GOSPEL AND THE FATHER'S TALK (GOD PRESENT)** Lecture Revelations of KING SOLOMON

SPIRITUAL LIBRARY and establish it physically in your houses. This is so that everybody would have these RECORDS. Go to read the books regularly. Every family should have a Library of **MY INFORMATION CENTRE** for their family members.

Every generation of a particular family should be able to easily go to their family Library of KING SOLOMON SPIRITUAL LIBRARY EVERLASTING GOSPEL and the **FATHER'S TALK (GOD PRESENT) Lecture Revelations** and read the Gospels and Lecture Revelations so that generations upon generations will access their KING SOLOMON SPIRITUAL LIBRARY.

You must all have **THE LIBRARY OF THE FATHER GOD ALMIGHTY** called **KING SOLOMON SPIRITUAL**

LIBRARY THE FATHER'S TALK (GOD PRESENT) LECTURE REVELATIONS in your homes and offices. The authorities and individuals concerned must see to that. When you establish your branch of KING SOLOMON SPIRITUAL LIBRARY and have the **EVERLASTING GOSPELS** and the **FATHER'S TALK (GOD PRESENT)** Lecture Revelations then that place is blessed and secured. In the name and Blood of Our Lord Jesus Christ, now and forever more, *Amien*.

THANK YOU FATHER

"THEUNISAL-SUREME SEACELION"
The Universal Supreme Season Celebration
=========
"THEUNI-SUREME WORA THECRO-THEUNISE"
The Universal Supreme Word Almighty
The Creator Of The Universe
==================
WWW.COME4WORD.COM

THE OFFICIAL SITE FOR

=============

EVERLASTING UNIVERSAL ALL WORD SEASON APPRECIATION CEREMONIAL PROGRAM

==========
THE UNIVERSAL SUPREME ALL WORD SEASON CELEBRATION (GOD PRESENT)

SOMETHING MORE THAN 'GOLD' THE HEART OF ALL MEN IS

WORD

==================

THE WORD IS THE MAKER, THE SOLE ADMINISTRATOR AND

THE CREATOR OF THE UNIVERSE THEREFORE, ALL HUMANKIND ON EARTH MUST APPRECIATE THE WORD IN ALL CAPACITIES FOREVER

=================

FROM EVERY OA OF AO TO AO OF AO (1st OCTOBER TO 10th OCTOBER). YEARLY IS THE UNIVERSAL SUPREME

ALL WORD SEASON CELEBRATION TO APPRECIATE

THE FATHER GOD ALMIGHTY
=================
CELEBRATION! CELEBRATION!! CELEBRATION!!!

THE UNIVERSAL SUPREME WORD CELEBRATION OF ALL TIME

THE ALMIGHTY FATHER GOD, THE CREATOR OF ALL

THINGS BROTHERHOOD

ORGANISED BY
KING SOLOMON SPIRITUAL LIBRARY

=======

HRM KING SOLOMON DAVID JESSE ETE
INSPIRATIONAL HEAD

IN THE HONOUR OF THE FATHER GOD THE CREATOR OF THE UNIVERSE THE HOLY SPIRIT OF TRUTH AND THE KING OF KINGS AND THE LORD OF LORDS

==========
THANK YOU FATHER

KING SOLOMON SPIRITUAL LIBRARY

THE GOD ENCYCLOPAEDIA WORD OF INFINITY

=============

King Solomon Spiritual Library, God Universal Information Centre
FATHER'S TALK (GOD PRESENT)

WITH LOVE

Covered: **This BOOK,** e-book, software or software's, books, websites, videos, audios, idea or ideas, formula or formulas, manual or instruction manual

... Hereby gives you a non-exclusive license to use the ... (THIS BOOK).

Some of the words here are coded with the (WORD OF SUPER HOLY AND INTELLIGENCE FATHER GOD ALMIGHTY)

Title, ownership rights, and intellectual property rights in and to the Website, Books, E-book, Audios and Videos, Shops and Store – e-Stores, Fundraisings,

Celebrations and the Supreme Word Seasons Celebration formulas and arrangements, Positive Inspiration, HOLY (FATA), FATHER GOD ALMIGHTY POSSESSING SPIRIT in thought, in words and in deed, thinking well, speaking well, hearing well and doing well shall remain in me and in ... The BOOK is protected by international copyright.

FATHER'S TALK (GOD PRESENT)

The message in **THE FATHER'S TALK (GOD PRESENT)** does not challenge any authority as individuals, groups or governments of any land or even any belief of any form. It is rather challenging the truth that is hidden from mankind. Therefore, any spirit, soul or physical human being who decides to challenge this truth shall have himself or herself to blame.

Key A: Any individual that reads any of **THE FATHER'S TALK** (GOD PRESENT) with faith; love and acceptance will experience immediate positive change in his or her life from spirit, soul to physical. If he or she accepts the message then he or she will be free from any evil.

Key B: **PEACE AND LOVE**
If you do not believe the contents of any of **THE FATHER'S TALK (GOD PRESENT)**, it is possible through **THE FATHER'S** divine love and peace to simply hand over your copy to a friend or somebody else

that would like to keep a copy, or by signing out from any of the websites that connect to **THE FATHER'S TALK (GOD PRESENT)** and KING SOLOMON SPIRITUAL e-LIBRARY without any evil and negative comments then you are blessed and free.

========

FROM THE DESK OF THE INSPIRATIONAL HEAD
Fees, Prices and Donations; There is no refund on fees, prices or donations since your fees, priced payments or donations are used as a charity contribution to do administrative work of **THE SUPREME WORD**, so please kindly read this first before you decide to involve yourself in any of the under mentioned of HRM King Solomon David Jesse **ETE** universal Inspirational Businesses

of (**GOD PRESENT**) in cash, kind and otherwise.

I CAME FROM THE FATHER GOD, WITH THE FATHER GOD, AND BY THE FATHER GOD TO ESTABLISH THE FOLLOWING:

THE FATHER'S TALK (GOD PRESENT), The Spiritual Advice, Healing and Counselling on General Live (The Universal Supreme Spiritual General Hospital), New Songs and Psalms of King David and Solomon, The Word of **GOD** Processing City in Ikot Okwo or e-City online, The Trinity Celebration, "**OUC FUND**", The Universal Bank Account For All Creations, "**ERUFA**" ETE Royal Universal Family, "**THEUNISAL-SUREME SEACELION**" The Universal Supreme Word Season Celebration To Appreciate **THE FATHER GOD ALMIGHTY** "**THEUNI-SUREME WORA**

The Supreme Celebration & Bylove of Word

THECRO-THEUNISE" The Universal Supreme Word Almighty, THE CREATOR OF THE UNIVERSE. Therefore all distributors and contributors should attach and make this information available to all readers, website visitors, distributors, affiliates person/group, celebrant and celebrations centres, supporters and promoters, members, workers and voluntary workers, Ete royal universal palace committee, governments and many other centres as an agreement. Please kindly know that I am not answering to any physical human except **PEACE, UNITY AND LOVE.**

"THEUNISAL-SUREME WORA THECRO-THEUNISE".

I AM IN THE STAGE OF SUPER HOLY AND INTELLIGENT FATHER GOD POSITIVE MADNESS OF THE HOLY SPIRIT OF TRUTH,
ENYEN ODUDU ODUDU ODUDU ABASI MI OOO ZIM ZIM ZIM ASSASU, POSITIVE POSITIVE POSITIVE. UKEMEKE AKA IDIOK UNAM.

Let the peace and blessing of THE HOLY FATHER abide with everyone who corporates with this divine **FATHER'S TALK (GOD PRESENT)**

THANK YOU FATHER
BY
THE HOLY SPIRIT OF
THE FATHER GOD
THROUGH HIS SERVANT
The Senior Christ Servant
HRM King Solomon David Jesse **ETE**
Brotherhood of the
Cross and STAR
Eteroyal Universal family

Ikot Okwo The Great City of Refuge,
Ete Community
Ikot Abasi LGA-543001
Akwa Ibom State Nigeria-W/A
Tel. 08036693841
Website: www.ksslibrary.com
Email: ksslibrary@eteroyalmail.com

==============

READ AT LEAST SEVEN LECTURE REVELATIONS BEFORE YOU CAN MAKE ANY COMMENTS

In the Name of Our Lord Jesus Christ, In the Blood of Our Lord Jesus Christ, Now and forever more

Everybody should have access to and read at least seven **FATHER'S TALK (GOD PRESENT)** Lecture Revelations before making any comments about it. If you do not go through at least seven

FATHER'S TALK Lecture Revelations and you comment, you may make mistakes. And when you make mistakes your blood will be upon you because you would have taken voluntary evolution to misquote **THE FATHER GOD THE CREATOR OF THE UNIVERSE**.

One of **THE FATHER'S TALK** stands for one SPIRIT of GOD, which means that THE **FATHER'S TALK** (**GOD PRESENT**) Lecture Revelations are witnessed by the Seven SPIRITS of GOD, which **I** use as the Seven Churches of GOD and Seven days of the Week, Seven spirits of Creation in one Supreme energy of **THE FATHER GOD**,

THE SPOKEN WORD therefore,

when you read seven **FATHER'S TALK** (**GOD**

PRESENT) Lecture Revelations then, **I, THE FATHER GOD** will reveal you as a positive person and then you will have a portion in **ME**. And one of **THE FATHER'S TALK** (**GOD PRESENT**) will have a portion in you. Then you would know that this information came from **THE FATHER GOD. THE FATHER'S TALK** (**GOD PRESENT**) is not a mere talk from a man!

In the Name of Our Lord Jesus Christ, In the Blood of Our Lord Jesus Christ, Now and forever more

THE UNIVERSAL INVITATION

====

You Are Invited To Join Me In THE UNIVERSAL SUPREME WORD SEASON CELEBRATION And Celebrate; Acknowledge, Appreciate and give full RECOGNITION to THE UNIVERSAL SUPREME WORD, YOUR LIFE, THE FORCE OF ALLTHINGS, THE TOTALITY OF ALL TOTALITIES YOUR CREATOR,

THE SUPREME FATHER GOD ALMIGHTY, THE CREATOR OF THE UNIVERSE Wherever You Be.

EVERY 1ST OCTOBER TO 10TH OCTOBER YEARLY

===

Published by:
**KING SOLOMON SPIRITUAL LIBRARY
ETEROYAL UNIVERSAL FAMILY
IKOT OKWO, ETE COMMUNITY**

IKOT ABASI L.G.A
AKWA IBOM STATE OF
NIGERIA
WEST AFRICA
WWW.KSSLIBRARY.COM
WWW.COME4WORD.COM
WWW.THEWORDCITY.COM
WWW.KINGSOLOMONSPIRITUALLIBRARY.COM

Contact EMAIL:
hrmkingsolomon@eteroyalmail.com

THANK YOU FATHER

The title List of some of the

FATHER'S TALK
(GOD PRESENT)

1: THE MANUAL OF THE SPOKEN WORD

2: THE MANUAL OF LIFE

3: INVESTMENT WITH GOD

4: ISO IBOT EDEM IBOT

5: THE CHARACTER OF THE NEW WORLD

6: HELPMANTRANS

7: UNDERSTANDING MY WORD

8: TRUTH, POSITION, POST AND NAME

9: NON STOP BLESSING

10: IMPRESSION

11: STAGES OF EDUCATIONS (SPE, SSE & SUE)

12: THE ENGINEERING OF LIFE

13: THE CONTENT PACKAGE

14: THE BUDGET OF THE NEW WORLD

15: DIVINE ATTENTION

16: THE BABY SPIRIT

17: PROMOTION

18: ADVANCE AND PROGRESSING MIND

19: THE TEMPLE OF THE LIVING GOD

20: I AM OK

21: THE SPIRIT OF TRUTH

22: THE PERFECT PERMANENCY

23: THE FATHER GOD, GOD, GOD THE FATHER

24: HUSBAND, WIFE AND CHILD

25: GOD AND HIS HARBINGER

26: LIFE EVERLASTING

27: POSSESS

28: MY MIND AND MY PLAN

29: AFTER HEART AND AFTER MIND

30: MY DECLARATION & STAND IN BCS

31: BEYOND THE HOPE OF FAITH

32: MENTAL STAIN

33: THE PRINCIPLE OF SELF HOLD

34: THE MASTERSHIP

35: HIDU-CUM

36: THE UNIVERSAL PARENT

37: ADVANCED YOU AND ME

38: THE GREAT UNIVERSAL CHANGE

39: THE PROJECTED MIND
40: INDESTRUCTIBLE BLESSED FIVE STARS

41: ASTROTS, GOD PRESENT I AND MY FATHER

42: SONGS THE COMPLETION

43: THE RIGHT BUTTON

44: AKWA ABASI IBOM- ETE - DIRECTING NDITO AKWA IBOM

45: THE DIGITAL AGE

46: GOD IS OFFICIAL CHAMPION

47: A TRUE WITNESS

48: MYSTERY OF PROCREATION AND BIRTH

49: THE UNIVERSAL UMBRELLA

50: THE FORERUNNER

51: A OF A TO Z (FIRST OF ALL)

52: MAN IN THREE CAPACITIES

53: THE TRUE LIFE OF HOLY SPIRIT PERSONIFIED

54: IN-BETWEEN THE FATHER & THE SON

55: DIVINE ARRANGEMENT & AUTHORITY

56: TWENTY FIRST CENTURY IS NOT FOR SATAN

57: THE SUPREME WORD SEASON CELEBRATION

58: THE MAXIMUM DEITY

59: TRANSFORMER TRANSMITTER AND WAVE

60: THE SUPREME FUTURE

61: THE BYLOVE OF WORD

62: THE SIGNATURE OF THE FATHER GOD

63: THE TWO WAYS

64: THE UNDERSTANDING OF LIFE

65: THE GREATER THAN SOLOMON IS HERE

66: THE CONQUEROR

67: THE SPIRITUAL GENERAL INSPECTOR OF LIFE

68: THE NIGERIA IN THE AFRICA Part one

**69: THE NIGERIA IN THE AFRICA
Part two**

70: THE CREATOR AND CREATIONS PART ONE

71: THE CREATOR AND CREATIONS PART TWO

72: THE CREATOR AND CREATIONS PART THREE

73: THE SUPREME TEACHER

74: THE SPIRITUAL COVER

75: THE NIGERIA IN THE AFRICA PART THREE

76: THE SUPREME BELIEVE

77: CAST AND BAN (LECTURE IN LIVERPOOL)

78: LIFE EXTENSION MANUAL

79: THE SPIRITUAL TRAFFIC

80: <u>THE VOICE OF THE CREATOR</u>

81: MY OFFICE

82: LIFE SPIRITUAL FIRE EXTINGUISHER

83: INFORMATION

84: FATHER GOD FINAL ARRANGEMENT

85: THE LOVERS OF CHRIST

86: I LOVE YOU, I LOVE YOU TOO

87: THE UNIVERSAL SUPREME UPDATE

88: THE SUPREME ALTAR

89: THE SOURCE AND DESTINATION

90: A SON LIKE THE FATHER THE KING OF KINGS A ROOTS FROM HEAVEN (NOT THIS TIME AROUND)

91: THE TRUE WITNESS AND THE TRUE SERVANT

92: THE FINAL ARRANGEMENT

93: A TRUE NIGERIAN MAN AND WOMAN

94: EVERYONE MUST PERSONALLY INVOLVE

95: BEWARE

96: ESIEN EMANA AKPAN "THE AFRICAN PROBLEMS"

97: THE SECRET OF THE UNIVERSAL PROBLEMS AND THE REMEDY (MUSLIM AND CHRISTIAN FROM THE SAME PARENT)

98: MMU-UDIM – THE BLESSED MOTHER (ABASI ME UDIM)

99: THINK WELL, SPEAK WELL AND DO WELL

100: THE STAGES OF HOW TO PROCESS THE WORD

101: EVIL STAIN, WHO RUNS AWAY FROM WHO

102: BEYOND HUMAN KNOW PURELY SPIRITUAL

103: THE INSPIRATIONAL WRITER

104: BIAKPAN OBIO AKPAN ABASI (THE NEW JERUSALEM CITY)

105: "OBAMA" THE STRAINTHEN AND THE SPIRIT OF BILL GATE AND MICROSOFT

106: THE HOLY TRINITY

107: AMEN –ODUWEM IKO ABASI

108: EVERYTHING – ALLTHINGS POSITIVE

109: OBLIGATIONS FOR ALL HUMAN BEINGS

110: MY EVERY REASON

THANK YOU FATHER

The Supreme Celebration & Bylove of Word

www.ingramcontent.com/pod-product-compliance
Lightning Source LLC
Chambersburg PA
CBHW021756230426
43669CB00006B/88